Facing up to Facebook

A survival guide for adoptive families

Eileen Fursland

Published by
British Association for Adoption & Fostering
(BAAF)
Saffron House
6-10 Kirby Street
London EC1N 8TS
www.baaf.org.uk

Charity registration 275689 (England and Wales) and SC039337 (Scotland)

© Eileen Fursland 2010

British Library Cataloguing in Publication Data
A catalogue record for this book is available from the British Library

ISBN 978 1 905664 98 6

Project management by Shaila Shah, Director of Publications, BAAF

Photograph on cover posed by models, by www.Istockphoto.com

Designed by Helen Joubert Design; typeset by Fravashi Aga

Printed in Great Britain by The Lavenham Press

Trade distribution by Turnaround Publisher Services, Unit 3, Olympia Trading Estate, Coburg Road, London N22 6TZ

BAAF is the leading UK-wide membership organisation for all those concerned with adoption, fostering and child care issues.

Contents

How this book came about

When BAAF first commissioned me to write about the impact of social networking on adoption, in late 2009, the plan was for three "pamphlets" on social networking websites and their role in contact issues with regard to adoption and fostering.

Shaila Shah, BAAF's Director of Publications, had realised that both parents and professionals, as well as adopted children and young people themselves, needed some information and advice on this issue.

Six months on, the "pamphlets" have turned into books - *Facing up to Facebook: A survival guide for adoptive families*, and *Social Networking and Contact: How social workers can help adoptive families*.

Why the transformation? Shaila and I quickly realised that pamphlets alone would not be enough to meet the huge need for information and advice on this issue. From the very beginning of my research, it became clear that social networking was having a huge impact on adoptive families and adoption professionals alike. I sent out an email to adoption social workers, via BAAF's network, which was circulated widely - I had a huge response, even receiving email replies from the United States and Australia. Social workers reported a steady stream of cases. The overriding message I received was: 'Thank goodness this is being addressed. I have no answers but I hope someone does.' One social worker said: 'I feel as though my role so far has been to run along behind with a mop.'

Adoption UK has a message board for adoptive parents. Messages posted there make clear the level of concern among parents about the risks of social networking for their adopted children. Adoption UK posted a request from me on its message board asking adoptive families to contact me if they had been affected by this issue. The parents who contacted me know, more than anyone, how important it is for adopted children and young people that we get this right.

My research showed that many adoptive families have concerns and some are struggling with the emotional consequences of situations thrown up by the use of social networking sites. Adoption professionals are facing completely new challenges and having to help and support families who find themselves in situations they never imagined. Many authorities have not yet developed guidelines and social workers are having to find ways of managing this complex issue as it affects more and more families.

BAAF quickly responded - Shaila agreed that instead of pamphlets we would publish two comprehensive books. BAAF arranged a conference to bring together IT and other professionals to discuss the issue. A third book - this time for foster carers, who are faced with different issues - is currently in production; a publication for young people will follow. Following on from the conference, BAAF hopes to run workshops for social workers and also publish a training pack, which can be used to deliver training on this issue to practitioners. BAAF's books, conference and training are timely and have been eagerly awaited.

The experiences of adoption practitioners and adoptive families inform every page of this book. If the book doesn't always provide neat answers, that's because it's rooted in real life, which can be messy. The many responses I received, the questions I was asked and everything I heard and read during the course of my research for this book showed me that this issue is of urgent relevance to everyone involved in adoption.

Acknowledgements

I would like to thank the social workers who told me about their experiences, passed on what they had learned or observed, and suggested questions for the book to address. The social workers (I can't thank them individually as many did not wish to be named, but they know who they are!) work in local authority adoption services in Anglesey, Bedfordshire, Berkshire, Brighton & Hove, Bristol, Bury, Cardiff, Cumbria, Edinburgh, Halton, Leicester, London (boroughs of Camden, Islington, Southwark, Havering and Harrow), Leeds, Luton, Manchester, Neath, North Yorkshire, Nottingham, Pembrokeshire, Reading, Sheffield, Stockport and Southampton.

Thanks to the adoptive parents who shared their experiences, wisdom and hard-won insights in the hope that these will help others. They took on the most difficult job in the world – being a parent to someone else's child – before anyone had ever heard of Facebook. And for some of them, the revolution in social networking has had unforeseen consequences, demanding reserves of strength, courage, patience and understanding that they could never have anticipated when they first adopted their child. I am deeply grateful to them. Thanks are also due to Adoption UK for offering to post my request.

Professionals from voluntary adoption agencies and other organisations also offered valuable input, including: Action for Children; Adoption UK; Child and Family Court Advisory and Support Service; Child Exploitation and Online Protection Service (CEOPS); Fever PR (for Facebook); Norwood; Our Place, Bristol; Thinking Allowed, Bristol; the Post-Adoption Centre, London; Respect; and Soldiers, Sailors, Airmen and Families Association.

Thanks are due to the following people for their help:

Lynda Gilbert, Adoption UK

Kate Richardson, CEOPS

Keitha Wakefield, Development Co-ordinator; and the North-East London Adoption Group

Norma Sargent, Coram Adoption Service

Susan Grindon, Assistant Team Manager; and the Post Adoption Team, Surrey County Council

I would also like to thank Alison Vincent (Adoption Consultant, Berkshire Adoption Advisory Service), Catherine Grace (Cabrini Children's Society) and Julia Venables (Adoption Team, Essex County Council) for the discussions on this issue; and Alison,

Catherine and Catherine Sturrock (Social Worker, Post Adoption Team, Essex County Council) for reading and commenting on the draft.

Thank you to everyone at BAAF who contributed to the book in any way:

Shaila Shah, Director of Publications, who originated the idea and commissioned the books, for her unfailing support.

Jo Francis, Editor, for preparing the scripts.

John Simmonds, Director of Policy, Research and Development and Elaine Dibben, Adoption Consultant, for reading and commenting on the drafts and for their many helpful suggestions.

John Simmonds, for contributing the Foreword.

Alexandra Conroy-Harris (Legal Consultant), Julia Feast (Policy, Research & Development Consultant), Katrina Wilson (Information Officer) and Lindsey Dunbar (Trainer, North-west Region), BAAF, for their expertise and input.

Although the book's title is *Facing up to Facebook,* it addresses all kinds of social networking and the advice given applies to other sites as well as Facebook. At the time of writing, Facebook is in the ascendancy, with 23 million UK users; in a few years, new sites may overtake Facebook and the technology will undoubtedly move on, presenting new opportunities and new challenges for us all. The advice, though, should still hold good.

I hope this book will help you and your adopted child.

Eileen Fursland

Note about the author

Eileen Fursland is a freelance writer. She writes mainly about social issues, particularly those affecting children. Eileen has contributed many articles to a range of magazines and newspapers, including *The Guardian*. She has written three books: *Children's Play*; *Working Mum's Handbook* (with Carole Smillie); and *Get Your Kids Fit!* (with Kelly Holmes), all published by Virgin Publishing; and an online reference source for anyone who works with children and young people, called *Understanding the Child* (to be published by Pearson Publishing Group in September 2010).

For BAAF, Eileen has authored or co-authored a number of books, guides and booklets, including *Caring for a Young Person who has been Trafficked: A guide for foster carers*, and a series of booklets on caring for unaccompanied asylum-seeking children and young people. She has written a series of training programmes with Kate Cairns (*Trauma and Recovery*; *Safer Caring*; *Transitions and Endings*; and *Building Identity*) as well as *Preparing to Adopt: A training pack for preparation groups* (with a BAAF working party).

Her most recent publications for BAAF are this book and a guide for social workers called *Social Networking and Contact: How social workers can help adoptive families*.

www.create-and-communicate.com

Foreword

Adoption has always been in a state of evolution and change. We have seen the nature of adoption radically change over the last 50 years, from one which provided a solution to society's negative attitudes to illegitimacy and single parenthood and unavailability of effective contraception and legal abortion, to one which provides a solution to serious issues arising from child maltreatment and parental risk and breakdown. Although both sets of circumstances focus on the child's lifelong need for a family, in which they are loved and belong, the circumstances in which the child is placed and the implications of this in the long term are now quite different. This is markedly so where the child is removed from his or her parent through legal proceedings instituted by the State and against the wishes of those parents, but even where consent is obtained, the actuality or likelihood of significant risk or harm to the child is likely to have played some part. However, although this is so in the UK, it is unlikely to be the case in many other countries where by far the greater number of adoptions are likely to be intercountry. The exception to this is the USA, where maltreated children placed for adoption, intercountry adoption and children relinquished by their parents exist alongside each other and which therefore presents a more complex picture.

As adoption has changed, so has the view that it was best kept a secret because it was a new start in life and that what went before was an unnecessary complexity in the child's view of who they were and what they were to become. While for some families secrecy was never an acceptable idea, others were confused and disturbed by what was recommended, and for yet others, it was something that they adhered to, with the adoption being disclosed to the child only much later or very late in life. But this then accepted view was challenged through the 1960s and 70s and families were advised that children should be told and the story of their adoption incorporated in a meaningful and sensitive way into family history and narrative. This started to include forms of contact – for some, confined to periodic exchanges of information; for others, more open forms of communication including direct contact. For adults the process was facilitated by the opening and availability of adoption records and support being available to find and make contact with birth parents and relatives. Similar opportunities were afforded to birth parents themselves. The complexity and emotion that such opportunities brought about were exquisitely demonstrated in Mike Leigh's film *Secrets and Lies*. Research by Feast, Howe and Triseliotis presented a more comprehensive evidence-based picture.

Such developments were not easily achieved and at the time there were fears that, if records were opened, there was potential for risk, particularly if adopted individuals were angry with birth parents about being given up for adoption. This fear was never realised in practice. Accompanying these developments was the recognition of just how significant children's curiosity about their adoption actually was and how enduring that could be. Commonly-asked questions included: Why was I adopted? Was there something

1

about me that made my birth parents give me up? Was I unlovable?, accompanied by others such as: Who are my birth parents? What do they look like? Would they love me more than you do? Not every child asked these questions and of course there were many other questions too. For some, the intensity of their curiosity never diminished. It may have been something that they kept to themselves or it may have been shared with a friend or with adoptive parents or other family members. For others, it may have come and gone and returned again at different points in their development and particularly in adolescence, or was something of little significance.

The part that indirect and direct forms of contact have played in the evolution of adoption has been highly significant. Ensuring that these arrangements between adoptive families and birth families are safe and in the child's best interests has rested in the mediating role of the adoption agency. If identifying information was to be withheld, then that would be the responsibility of the adoption agency and managed by them. If information was to be exchanged and identifying information withheld, then the exchange of information would need to happen through the adoption agency. If there were changes of circumstances and a request to change arrangements, then this would be mediated by the adoption agency. This is not to say that adoptive families and birth families didn't or don't make these arrangements themselves directly, without going through the adoption agency - some do, although we know little about this. But the role of the adoption agency in managing, mediating and arranging links between adoptive families and birth families cannot be underestimated. And this has become even more pronounced as adoption has come to involve children who have been maltreated. The management of risk, keeping the child safe, and maintaining the integrity and functioning of the adoptive family are continuing responsibilities of the agency. That is not to say that all birth parents continue to pose a risk - many certainly do not. But the agency always has a responsibility to ensure, wherever it can, that confidentiality of identifying information is maintained and the nature, frequency and amount of information exchanged is manageable for the child and adopters. These issues change over time in individual cases and sometimes in unplanned or unpredictable ways, but the agency has a primary responsibility to ensure that the placement is secure and the child's needs met.

And then we have the advent of social networking sites and prominent among them all is Facebook. Social networking allows people to exchange information with little effort, find people they have lost contact with, and establish new "friends" in ways that were previously unthought of. It has had a significant impact on the notion of social identity, personal relating and relationships and privacy. It has provided new ways for people to communicate but it has posed risks to privacy and provided new opportunities for exploitation of the vulnerable.

It is clear that many of these issues have impacted on adoption. They have developed fairly rapidly as social networking has developed rapidly, but recently the issues have suddenly gathered momentum and it is now clear that many people - adopted children and their adoptive parents, birth parents and other birth family members - and adoption agencies have been profoundly affected by the ease, directness and opportunities social networking sites make available. Social networking allows individuals to circumvent the agency's established role in preserving confidentiality, mediating information exchange and providing guidance and support. It has resulted in breaches of confidentiality and unexpected, unplanned and unthought-through contact resulting in distress, anxiety and unsettled young people and adoptive parents. It is a serious and worrying development. There are also examples where it has provided opportunity for the exchange of information in constructive, helpful and enriching ways.

What is clear is that something significant has changed about adoption through the advent of social networking and there is no going back on this. Some of the discussion that has occurred suggests that adoption needs to fundamentally change. Other people believe that, as adoption has always done, it needs to adapt. What is clear is that there is no question that any adoptive family, birth family or adoption agency can ignore social networking. Policy and practice will need to develop to ensure that all the advantages that adoption brings continue to be available to those children who need it. It should not and must not be undermined by social networking.

Eileen Fursland has been the first to explore the nature of people's experience of the impact of social networking sites in adoption and, in gathering that information together, has identified a number of important issues that are likely to inform adoption practice in years to come. What started out as a brief by BAAF to write guidance turned into a major journey of discovery. Eileen was told about many experiences involving social networking that have affected adopted young people and their families and birth relatives. Sometimes the lessons to be learned are clear; sometimes questions remain. Some of the experiences told to Eileen were disturbing and upsetting, others indicated where important lessons had been learnt. Eileen has pulled all of this together in an important guide that is groundbreaking in its significance. There is no doubt that there is more to be learnt as the issues evolve, but there couldn't be a firmer ground on which to do so.

John Simmonds, Director of Policy, Research and Development, BAAF

May 2010

Why you need this book

The world of adoption contact, search and reunion has changed. Adoptive families
- and adoption workers - are facing unprecedented challenges and dilemmas. Why?
The "social" use of the internet has had a huge impact on society and the way people
communicate with one another. Social networking sites such as Facebook have made
finding and contacting people easier than ever before. This has had an impact on many
adoptive families already and has the potential to affect many more.

Increasingly, young people are using Facebook and other websites to trace and contact
their birth parents and other birth relatives. Birth relatives, in turn, are using the internet
to trace their children. Once they have made contact, adopted young people may go on
to have phone calls and even meetings with their birth parents or brothers and sisters -
often in secret.

Knowing about their birth relatives is undeniably important for many adopted children,
but unplanned direct contact, through Facebook or other sites, bypasses the support
and safeguards that are usually in place. At its worst, such contact can destroy trust and
have significant emotional repercussions for everyone concerned.

If you are an adoptive parent, you may already be aware of the risks involved and you
may be wondering what, if anything, you can or should do. Or perhaps your child has
not yet started using the internet, but you are already concerned about protecting his
identity online and want to know how to manage this when the time comes.

In the age of social networking, much of the conventional wisdom, advice and guidance
in relation to tracing, contact and reunion in adoption seems to miss the point. Facebook
has blown it out of the water. Local authorities and voluntary adoption agencies, as
well as adoptive families, are quickly having to get to grips with a new reality. This book
looks at the way the internet, social networking and other technologies are changing
the landscape of adoption contact, search and reunion. It also tries to map out this new
landscape to help you to find your own route through it.

You may think that the answers must lie in controlling your child's use of the internet.
Perhaps you feel that, because you don't know much about computers, you are
powerless to protect your child or manage what they do online. It clearly helps if you
do understand the internet and how to protect your child's online identity, but this will
not help in a situation where a young person is determined to do things in his own way
- especially if he decides not to tell you. However expert you are in using computers, if
your child is actively looking for his birth parents or is already in contact with them and
you are unaware of this, you will be faced with a major challenge at some point.

So this book addresses internet safety and how to protect your child's identity online.
But it also looks at some of the more complex issues of communication, relationships
and identity and the difficult balancing act between responding to your child's desire

to know more and growing need for autonomy and protecting him (sometimes, from himself).

This guide doesn't provide any easy answers but it does include hard-won insights from adoptive parents and adoption workers who have had to face up to the impact of Facebook.

I hope this book will help you become better informed and better prepared, so that you and your adopted child or teenager can steer a safer course through whatever lies ahead.

Note

Please note that I have alternated the use of "he" and "she" throughout, for example, in Chapter 1 I use he, in Chapter 2 she, and so on. All references, of course, apply to both sexes.

Please note also that where names have been used in case examples, these have all been changed to protect confidentiality.

Eileen Fursland

The importance of openness

Many people who adopted a young child, who has now become a teenager, didn't expect that their child would have any direct contact with their birth parents until he was an adult – and only then if he wanted it, chose it and it was properly managed.

But everything has changed since the explosion in social networking. Children who were adopted as babies or toddlers and are now teenagers are growing up with Facebook as a central and readily available part of their lives. Now, it is relatively easy for adopted children and young people to find and make direct contact with their birth family – without having to ask anyone else. This has never been the case before.

All adoptive parents need to realise that, in the Facebook age, it is quite likely that a child with unanswered questions or a yearning curiosity about their birth family will one day decide to look for answers on the internet. Or they may find that their child has been contacted via Facebook out of the blue by a birth brother or sister, mother or father or other family member. In many adoptive families this has happened already.

If you adopted your child before anyone had even heard of Facebook, you may be feeling that you didn't sign up for this. Many adoptive parents are struggling from the impact already; others are worried about what might happen in their family.

This shouldn't be something that you put off thinking about until your child starts using the internet. You need to start thinking about this whether your child is 14 or only four and whether you adopted your child years ago or are at the beginning of the adoption journey.

Staying connected

You will have learned in your adoption preparation course about the importance of life story work and contact with birth family members, and their role in helping the child with his sense of who he is. It is likely that, at the time of the adoption, there was a plan and an agreement for letterbox contact with your child's birth family or even some face-to face-contact. You know about the importance of continuity, of helping your child to develop a positive identity and of answering their questions about adoption in a way appropriate for their age. You understand that your child has another family, and that this is important in a number of ways as a part of their identity and the development of their self-esteem.

Many adoptive parents know all this and work hard to build this into their family life. The child comes to understand more about the realities of why he was adopted and is pleased to hear about his birth parents. In many instances, the original plans change or circumstances alter. Sometimes, these are changes for the better and enhance the security and wellbeing of the child and everybody else involved. In other circumstances,

6

changes become difficult. Perhaps the birth parents lead difficult lives and stop collecting or responding to letters or don't turn up to meetings when these are arranged. Perhaps you feel that your child isn't getting anything out of the contact or is very upset by it.

Sometimes adoptive parents find contact with birth parents harder than they thought they would, once they become attached to the child and start to think of him as theirs. They may also develop a deeper understanding of how their child has been affected by his early experiences before adoption and this can lead to them feeling ambivalent about writing with news about how the child is doing. Contact can sometimes be difficult to arrange or fit into your life. At times you may wonder why you are bothering.

> *With very young children it may seem to adopters that contact meetings are of little point or value to the child as he or she is not asking questions about adoption. What is likely to help such adopters persist with contact is an understanding that the child will need to address questions of identity in the future. In my research, adopters who showed a good understanding of the lifelong needs of their child were more highly motivated to sustain contact as they had long-term goals in mind.*
>
> NEIL, 2002

Maintaining letterbox or direct contact, over the years, is more important than it may seem at the time. If your child has questions about their birth family later on, it is a way to find the answers they need. Some adoptive parents don't like sharing the birth parents' letters with their child or don't feel it will help him. But sharing information with your child does serve a purpose. It shows him that you know that this is important and that you yourself have accepted this information. It shows him that, even when information is difficult, you have the emotional resources to cope even if you may not like it. It also creates a sense that, even when issues are painful, it is better to share and talk about them and that they don't need to be kept a secret because you might be upset.

Creating an atmosphere of openness in which to talk about and work on upsetting and difficult issues is a crucial part of all family life – and, with its own particular issues, this is equally true in adoption. It needs to be built into the core of the way that your family works. It is never easy but if you persevere, it could save you and your child much heartache later on.

CASE STUDY

A few years ago an 11-year-old girl emailed adoption services, saying that she had been thinking about her birth mother and did not have any information about her and asked if we could send her some information. My manager emailed her back saying we would need to speak to her parents, which we did. Her adoptive parents were very surprised, saying they were open with her. They had received letterbox news from her birth father since her placement, but not the birth mother and her whereabouts were unknown.

Coincidentally, the birth mother contacted me only a few months later to say she was back in the area and asking for help to write a letter and send photos. I contacted the adoptive parents and they agreed. For the last few years we have sent on the birth mother's letters.

Last year I had reason to speak to the adoptive parents with a concern about contact, to be told that they had not shared any of the letters sent by the birth parents with their daughter, now aged nearly 16.

So, even when people say they are open, they are sometimes not, and sometimes they do not understand or want to understand that their children will be curious. I have to question what messages they have been given in their training.

An adoption social worker

CONTACT WITH BIRTH RELATIVES

For most adopted children, their birth family will be present in their mind throughout their lives. Sometimes this may be in the forefront and sometimes it may be in the background. The child may think about his birth family in ways that are helpful or unhelpful to him. Direct or indirect forms of contact may facilitate this or not. Just because a child never brings up the subject does not mean that he is not thinking about it or that he won't find himself thinking about it in the future.

- The purpose of contact is not to help or to appease the birth parents – its purpose is primarily to benefit the child.

- In letterbox contact, the adoptive parents write to the child's birth parent, giving them news about the child. The birth parents or other relatives may also write to the adoptive parents. The information is passed through the adoption agency to maintain confidentiality and mediate on any potentially difficult issues.

- The birth parents should not be given any information through the adoption agency that would compromise the adoptive family's anonymity.

- Sometimes there is face-to-face contact between brothers and sisters who are placed in different families, if this is seen as being in the children's best interests. In some placements, there may be face-to-face meetings between the child and birth parent.

- Contact arrangements are usually made under a voluntary agreement.

It's not about you - your child's curiosity is natural!

It is normal, natural and healthy for adopted children to be curious about their birth parents and their brothers and sisters, to wonder what they are like, and even to wish they could meet them. Sometimes adoptive parents feel hurt or threatened by the child's need to know. Try to remind yourself: *It's not about you.*

Questions of "identity" come sharply into focus as children reach adolescence. All adolescents start to wonder about who they really are, what has shaped them and how others see them. Adopted young people have more questions and experience more confusion than many of their peers because - emotionally - they are members of *two* families. There is a natural urge to find out about their origins and fill in the gaps. This is why life story work that was appropriate when the child was three or four will need to be updated as the child's needs and curiosity develop. Even when they have been told everything that is known about their past, they may still develop a strong need to know what is happening to their birth parents and/or brothers and sisters *now*.

> *I am aware of one case of a 14-year-old leaving her adoptive home and disappearing to live with her birth father (but in this case I know that the adopters did not respond a few years earlier when she had questions about her birth family, so it could have been curiosity getting the better of her)...Good communication between adopters and their child sounds obvious, but frankly I see cases of children unable to ask poignant questions as their development and understanding increase.*
>
> A POST-ADOPTION SOCIAL WORKER

For young people who were adopted, particularly if they suffered neglect or abuse in early life, the teenage years are often turbulent. Relationships with their adoptive family can become strained, sometimes to breaking point. Just like other teenagers, adopted teenagers test boundaries, can appear to reject their parents, trigger family rows, and feel like running away. But there is an added dimension to all of this for an adopted teenager - the idea that his birth family is somewhere out there.

> *It was just so easy for our daughter to find her birth parents on Facebook – almost too tempting. It is so easy for children to get on these sites and look for people without really understanding the possible consequences for all involved. Adopted children often have multiple problems, and are often looking for "something else" in their lives, no matter how happy and loved they've been in their adoptive families. Finding their "other" family on Facebook can probably seem like the answer to some of them but will almost certainly cause them much heartache in the long run.*
>
> AN ADOPTIVE MOTHER

It can be important for an adopted child's self-esteem to know that his birth parents care and want to see him.

The fact that my daughter's birth father searched for her meant the world to her – even though he is a schizophrenic who is in secure accommodation and she was told that it would be dangerous for her to have contact with him. There is a powerful pull, particularly in teens, to either make contact or at least get some up-to-date information. Unattached teens seem to need to make sense of who and why they are as they are, and are usually not getting on well with – or sadly are even estranged from – their adoptive families by that time.

Teenagers (adopted or birth children) who have formed an attachment to their parents "know" they hate their parents, know they will NEVER be like their parents and generally find their parents a pain in the bum...they are secure in all of that. No matter how horrible the teen years may be, they can safely kick against their family, knowing and feeling secure that all will be well and that they "belong".

If only unattached teens could be helped to articulate all their angst and feelings...how different the outcomes could be for them. They make so many mistakes at this time in their life, during a period when they just don't feel like they "belong" anywhere.

AN ADOPTIVE MOTHER

Why your approach is important

You won't always know if your child has questions about his past or is curious about his birth family. He may keep his questions to himself, either because that's the way he operates or because he thinks you don't want to talk about it or will be angry or hurt. Sometimes family life gets in the way - the demands of work, school, homework, out-of-school activities and everyone's social lives can crowd other things out. So, if your child doesn't bring it up himself, adoption and birth family can easily become subjects that are never talked about.

A lot of adoptive parents are inhibited when it comes to talking about the child's past. They tend to say, 'My child knows they can ask me anything they want and I'll tell them'. But that may not happen – the child may never ask. Parents understandably push it to the back of their minds.

We say to parents that, in our experience, every adopted child does think about it.

AN ADOPTION SOCIAL WORKER

Try to share with your child the letters you receive from his birth parents through letterbox contact, unless there is a good reason not to.

Some parents have a high tolerance threshold for letters that are signed "Mummy" or that say things like "I miss you", while others feel threatened and won't show them to the child.

AN ADOPTION SOCIAL WORKER

If you are unhappy about the content of the letters, discuss it with the person who manages the letterbox contact.

Many adoptive parents and adoption professionals believe that, if a child has always been able to ask about and discuss and think about what he wants to know about his past, he is less likely to search for information in secret on the internet.

Life story work

Local authorities are required by statutory guidance to include an adopted child's birth parents' first names and the birth family surname in the life story book, so this is standard practice. However, these and other details can allow the child to search for his parents online. Some parents and professionals have anxieties about this, which have led them to feel that practice should change and the child's surname should be kept separately from the life story book rather than in it; that way, parents can gauge the best time to tell the child this. However, others feel that leaving the surname out of the life story book gives the wrong message and will simply make the child more curious about what else is being kept from him. They believe that doing this does not take account of the value to the child of knowing about his past. Each child's case needs to be assessed individually and decisions should be based on the specific details of his family and the circumstances. Decisions on any precautions like this should be proportionate to the risks presented.

Social workers are also required to prepare a "later life letter", which gives a fuller picture of the circumstances which led to the adoption than the simple version in the life story book. They give this to the adoptive parents before the adoption order is made. You can give this to your child when you feel the time is right or when he wants more information.

Tell the truth, even if it hurts

Many parents' inclination is to protect their child from the truth about what happened to him in his early years. But – even though parents are acting out of an understandable wish to protect – children have a need to know. They need to be told in a way that is realistic, helpful and supportive. It is an important part of developing an adoption identity.

Exploring the reality of his birth family and the circumstances of his adoption is not something that any child should go through without support. Far better that your child hears the truth from you in the right way rather than discovering it when he finds documents and reports while you're out, goes digging around on the internet, or is told by a birth brother or sister during a secret late-night session on the computer.

> The internet is the first point of reference for most young people when there is something they want to know. Young people in Britain turn to the internet to look for help with personal problems rather than seek advice from their parents or friends, according to a survey published in March 2010.
>
> Nine out of 10 of the 1,000 under-25s told the survey for national free helpline Get Connected that they had used the web to search for help in solving a personal problem.
>
> Only one-third said they would turn to their mother to discuss a problem, while just one in 20 would speak to their father. Half said they would be likely to speak to a friend.

Children are capable of using the internet to search for information at a young age. This may mean telling your child some things before you would otherwise choose to.

How much do you tell? Of course it is not easy to talk to children about the details. It hurts to remind your child of the pain and distress of his early life or in his birth parents' life, or just how he was harmed and by whom. And you will have learned in adoption preparation groups that "demonising" the birth parents could harm the child's self-esteem, given that he is genetically related to them. This sometimes leads adoption workers and adoptive parents to skate over the harsh reality, from the best of motives. The child hears messages like: 'Your parents really loved you, but they couldn't look after you.'

Children who have never known their birth parents sometimes develop an idealised view of them. If they have never been told the facts, when they reach an age when they could seek out and make contact with their birth parents (or be contacted by them), they may be faced with complex and disturbing issues. They may struggle to make sense of what they hear or refuse to believe it.

> *Some children are sensible and realistic about what they can expect from their birth parents. It helps if you have discussed it openly from an early age, so the birth parents are not surrounded by a sense of mystery and your child will not have a fantasy about what life would have been like with the birth parents.*
>
> AN ADOPTION SOCIAL WORKER

How much you tell and how you phrase it will of course depend on your child's age, but you do need to provide a sensitive, honest and open account of what happened to your child when they were with their birth family.

> *You are bringing your child up in a loving, safe environment. If he was adopted while very young, a loving, safe environment is all he will be able to remember. When you tell a child 'your parents could not keep you safe', does he really know what that means or what his early life was really like? He may have no real understanding of what you mean. You need to tell them more and more as they get older, and by the time they are teenagers, they need to understand everything.*

AN ADOPTION SOCIAL WORKER

There may come a time when your child learns that you have kept certain information from him. Think carefully about any information you are not sharing. One day he may want to know why.

> *They [my adoptive parents] knew about her all along. I was so upset when I found out, because I didn't know they knew.*

AN ADOPTED 16-YEAR-OLD WHO WAS CONTACTED BY HER HALF-SISTER ON FACEBOOK

Perhaps you were never given much information yourself at the time of the adoption? See Chapter 2, *Finding out more and re-opening contact*.

What can and should you do, right now?

- Stay connected with the birth family if contact has been agreed.
- Talk openly about your child's adoption and birth relatives *within the immediate family*.
- Don't wait for your child to bring up the subject.
- Tell the truth in a way appropriate for your child's age.
- Remember that his need for information will grow as he develops.

In the section titled *Finding out more*, we list some books that will help you talk to your child about adoption and tell them the truth about their origins.

Outside the family, you should be careful to keep your child's personal details private. From the very start, make sure that you and your child are doing everything possible – both on the internet and in the real world - to reduce the risk that a birth relative could trace you.

If there is to be any direct contact with your child's birth family, it is far better that it comes at a time when you and your child have chosen it and are ready for it. Chapters 5, 6 and 7 tell you more about protecting your privacy online and offline.

Finding out more and re-opening contact

Even if you've talked about the past, one day your child may want to know what is happening in her birth parents' lives *now*. And even if you have been careful to maintain contact and share letters, there may come a time when that information is not enough.

If your child has always felt able to ask you what she wants to know, then – with a bit of luck – when that time comes, she will come to you with her questions. That means you have the chance to help and give support in finding out the answers.

> *Reassure your child that you are not hurt, insulted or rejected by her action (or desire, if it has not happened yet) and that any anxiety comes from concern, not criticism or fear of the birth family.*

ANDREW LISTER, CONSULTANT CLINICAL PSYCHOLOGIST

If your child has expressed an interest in finding out more about her birth parents or perhaps even meeting them, where do you go from here?

- First, you need to discuss this and, together, work out what your child wants. They may not even be sure of this themselves. Sometimes children express a desire to meet their birth mother when what they actually mean is: 'I want to know more about my birth mother.' If they have the opportunity to discover the information indirectly now, they may decide to leave any direct contact until they are older.

You may be able to:

- Show the child her "later life letter" – the letter written by the birth parents/social worker at the time of the adoption. It gives a more adult explanation about the circumstances of the adoption, to be given to the child when old enough to understand.

- Ask the adoption agency if they could look again at the adoption files and tell you what was known about the birth parents.

- Find out if the adoption agency has continued contact with the birth parents.

- Look into the possibility of setting up some letterbox contact now, if appropriate.

- Build on letterbox contact, if you have kept this up.

- Ask the adoption agency to write to the birth parent to ask for up-to-date information.

- Ask the adoption agency to arrange a meeting between your child and a birth relative – if it's appropriate, if both parties want it, and after a period of considering and preparing for this.

Sometimes, at the time of the adoption, birth parents are refused any contact because this is not considered to be in the child's best interests. But, over the years, some people do change, mature and sort out their lives. And what is in the child's best interests can also change.

Have "what if...?" conversations

You both need to be prepared for what might happen. Try to get your adopted child or teenager to share their thoughts and feelings with you.

You could, for instance, ask them about what they would do if:

- they wanted to know more about their birth relatives;
- they wanted to contact the birth relatives, perhaps even to get in touch;
- a birth sibling or half-sibling contacted them on Facebook;
- the birth mother or birth father contacted them on Facebook;
- someone came up to her in the street and named the birth mother or father and asked if she was their daughter.

Is there a risk that talking about finding birth relatives on Facebook could perhaps put the idea into their head? This is possible, of course. But simply ignoring these worrying possibilities carries risks too. How to play it is a tough decision that every adoptive parent now has to make, and there are no right answers. You and your partner, if you have one, may want to make use of other sources of support, including the adoption agency, to think this through.

Try to get your child to think about the possible outcomes of making contact in different ways. Show them that you are interested and curious about what could happen and where it could lead. Perhaps you could talk about the following.

- Family relationships can be complicated. Is your child assuming that birth relatives will automatically welcome direct contact? Remind her that it may come as a shock to them. Birth parents may have all sorts of issues in their own lives that you don't know about (as well as the ones you do).

- To have a child turn up in their lives out of the blue could have serious repercussions for some birth parents (see pp. 29–30).

- Going about it in the right way and making the initial approach through the adoption agency gives the person time to think and absorb the news rather than reacting instantly – the outcome is likely to be more positive.

- Even though your child may think she can handle it, there's no way of controlling the way things might develop – it could snowball in a way that she didn't expect.

Teenagers, however, have always demanded the right to make their own mistakes. Sometimes they will do risky or frankly dangerous things, no matter what you do or say.

Re-opening contact: how to manage it

The birth parents may be known to the agency through letterbox contact, for example, or because there are continuing issues with other children. Or it may be that no one from the local authority or agency has had contact with the birth parents for some years.

If you don't have much information about your child's life story, or want up-to-date information about the birth parents, approach the adoption agency. They will discuss the options with you and advise on possible courses of action. If it is possible to get more information, they can work with you on the process of initiating some indirect contact.

Before any such contact, you may want to know – if it's possible to find out – how the birth parent(s) views the adoption now. Have they accepted it? Do they have a sense of responsibility or are they angry with children's services for taking their child away?

- Offer to arrange for your child to talk to somebody outside the family. It may make things easier for all of you if she can talk to an experienced adoption social worker who can explain and explore the issues.

- Whatever plan you make, give your child some space to think things through.

- Some young people become even more determined if they think you are opposed to something they want to do. You may well feel apprehensive and threatened at the thought of your child meeting the birth parents. You may be afraid of where it will lead, of letting them back into your child's life, of losing your child to them. Try to listen to what your child is telling you about her needs and wishes rather than your own fears.

- Adopted people have a right to know about their own family. So the questions are "what is the best way?" and "when is the right time?", not whether your child should know or not. (This is different from a discussion you might have about drugs, for example.) Timing is a grey area, on which you and your teenager may have differing views. You need to discuss this, while respecting your teenager's point of view.

- If a decision is made, after a full discussion, to try to establish direct contact, and this seems possible, then you need to think carefully about how, when and where this is to happen and who should be present. An adoption support worker could facilitate at a meeting between you and the birth parent(s), if appropriate.

- Don't push to be involved in every aspect of the contact – for instance, tell your child that you would not necessarily expect to be there when they meet the birth parents, but that you will help to arrange it, including transport.

- Making contact may seem risky and certainly in some cases it seems the wrong thing to do. In some circumstances, birth relatives pose a risk and you would not wish to encourage or facilitate any contact between them and your child. The social worker should carry out a risk assessment in these situations, which will inform whether and how contact should be arranged.

- However, it is also risky if a young person searches and finds their birth family and initiates contact on their own when you have no chance of helping them manage the situation. So, after a risk assessment, it is important that adults explain what they know and give the young person the reasons for their decisions.

Try to ensure your son or daughter has a good understanding of the complexities of making contact with their birth relatives and where it could lead.

Sometimes, adoptive families who have had successful indirect contact over a period of time are happy to make the contact direct, for instance, with phone calls and perhaps even face-to-face meetings. Emails, instant messaging and social networking sites sometimes prove useful channels for this kind of contact between adoptive and birth families or the child and a birth relative, where the contact has been planned and agreed.

> *We have been working on one case in which there has been positive and well-established indirect contact between the adoptive parents and birth parents. Recently the adoptive mum said to me: 'I think we should exchange phone numbers'. So I met the birth parents and discussed boundaries, then I took their email addresses and the adoptive mother and her child emailed them. You have to think it through like a contact agreement.*
>
> AN ADOPTION SOCIAL WORKER

Going through the agency or going it alone?

Some adoptive parents know the birth parents' names and sometimes they themselves have even looked them up and found them on Facebook. They feel that this is a useful source of information for them and their child. It would be unwise in most circumstances to try to make contact without first exploring this with the adoption agency and an experienced adoption social worker.

Adopted teenagers may not see it that way. They may be excited and impatient and incapable of containing their urge to get in contact, especially if they have already traced their birth relative through Facebook. Going through the "proper channels" means having to wait, and this can be a lot to ask.

Some adoptive parents manage contact with their child's birth relatives directly, without the involvement of the adoption agency, and have found that internet contact can be positive and beneficial.

CASE STUDY
....

Our experience of the internet and contact has been very positive as it allows communication in an intimate but controlled way between the adults involved. We have two adopted children, now 9 and 11, from different parents. We spent years trying to make direct contact with the birth mother of the older boy with enormous obstruction from social services and other agencies.

Eventually the birth mum found us via Google – she must have had more information to go on than we realised. We were able to move gradually from email contact between myself and the birth mother, to face-to-face contact, again between the adults involved to get to know one another, and then with the children (birth mother and son, various siblings and other relatives). While we do have phone numbers, I can see that it is still hard for the birth mother to contact us directly and email continues to be a good, fairly neutral way of exchanging information. She does have a Facebook account but it doesn't seem to be active.

Our son knows that he can email, phone or write to his mother at any time, and knowing that has been enough; so far at least, he has never wanted to, being very glad that I can keep the contact and make arrangements on his behalf. I print off everything and keep it for him as some way of compensating for the many years when we were told that she did not want contact and had not tried to write (not true as it turned out).

With our younger son, contact was with the adoptive parents of two of his younger siblings. Again, for some reason entirely opaque to us and the other parents, the social workers and agencies involved tried hard to prevent any contact between us.

When we were told that face-to-face contact with them could jeopardise the placement, we were able to keep up email contact and, once the adoptions were finalised, move to regular face-to-face contact – again this has been 100 per cent beneficial for everyone involved.

I see that our younger son's birth mother also has a Facebook account, but again, not active.

This could be a potential means of direct contact and one that I would welcome, but I am very careful not to post anything relating to the children or other identifying information, such as where we live, on Facebook.

An adoptive mother

··

Should you initiate this before your child is 18?

Finding out more about birth parents and even asking for contact, through the agency or local authority, can be initiated at any time – you don't have to wait until your child is 18.

If you start before your child has reached the stage when she is confident enough to do this independently, she may be more willing to accept your help.

Children and young people can approach adoption support services themselves if they don't want you to be involved.

If this happens before the young person is 18, social workers will keep you informed and work alongside you while they are preparing and supporting all parties through any reunion. But at 18, young people are treated as adults, so if your child does not initiate contact until then and chooses not to tell you about it when she does, you will be out of the loop.

ADOPTION CONTACT REGISTERS

Adopted people and birth relatives can register on an adoption contact register, a service which enables adopted people and birth relatives who want to contact one another to register that fact, and be put in touch if both have registered. The arrangements vary from country to country within the UK depending on where the adoption took place. The adoption charity AAA NORCAP also has a separate adoption contact register for adopted people and birth relatives. Contact details for all the country-specific adoption contact registers can be found at the end of this book.

VETOES

If a person was adopted before 30 December 2005, then there is a facility for them to register a qualified or an absolute veto (in regard to being contacted) with the appropriate adoption agency (the agency that arranged the adoption). However, the facility to register a veto only applies to people who were adopted in England and Wales.

MAKING CONTACT AND INTERMEDIARY SERVICES

Adopted people in England and Wales can obtain a copy of their original birth certificate when they are aged 18 years. The original birth certificate contains identifying information which can help adopted people begin a search for birth family members. However, the arrangements for obtaining a copy and also requesting access to adoption records held by the adoption agency are different depending whether or not you were adopted before or after 30 December 2005. This is referred to as pre- and post-commencement adoptions, following the implementation of the Adoption and Children Act 2002.

Adopted people in Northern Ireland can also obtain a copy of their original birth certificate at the age of 18. In Scotland, adopted people have the same right when they reach 16.

BAAF operates www.adoptionsearchreunion.org.uk, a website which provides information on locating adoption records, along with a searchable database of adoption support and intermediary services.

Birth relatives and requests for reunion

Regulations governing adoptions that took place before 30 December 2005 in England and Wales set out that, once an adopted child is over 18, the birth relatives have the right to request an intermediary service with a view to making indirect contact. There are different legislative frameworks for providing intermediary services for birth relatives, depending on whether the adoption order was made pre- or post-commencement.

Birth relatives in Northern Ireland and Scotland can either contact the agency that arranged the adoption to find out if they are able to offer an intermediary service, or seek advice from relevant services (see *Find out more*).

The agency they approach to provide an intermediary service has to assess the application and decide whether or not it should go ahead. If the agency is not the same one that was involved in the adoption, it has to contact the adoption agency to seek its views about whether it should provide an intermediary service. Birth relatives are not automatically entitled to have an intermediary service approach the adopted person on their behalf. In some circumstances, the intermediary agency may decide it is not appropriate to offer the service.

The intermediary service, usually an adoption worker with expertise in this area, would contact the adopted adult and ask whether they would welcome contact. The choice is for the adopted adult to make. They can say whether or not they want to take things further. Going through an intermediary service provides support and safeguards both parties' privacy and contact details.

In both cases, things proceed slowly, step by step, with preparation and support for both parties from the intermediary before any face-to-face contact is arranged. At any stage, the adopted adult can say no to any further contact. The intermediary keeps the contact details secret, and acts as a "buffer" between the two parties.

Adopted people and reunion

Adopted people aged 18 or over (in England, Wales and Northern Ireland) can find out about their birth family if they want to; in Scotland, adopted people can do so when 16. They can:

- apply for a copy of their original birth certificate;
- get help from an intermediary agency to find out about their background and, if they want to, ask the agency to approach their birth relatives on their behalf.

My adopted daughter went through conventional social service channels, with my support and intervention, to "find" her birth family information at the stroke of midnight on her 18th birthday! Guess she was looking for a rainbow's end...

AN ADOPTIVE MOTHER

Adopted adults are entitled to counselling and support and to use an intermediary service to make the initial approach.

Of course, adopted people don't magically become emotionally mature, sorted and stable overnight, when they reach a certain age. Reunion with birth parents can be a stressful and emotional experience whenever it happens.

An adopted person tracing birth parents is still likely to need emotional support from her adoptive parents. If she is to turn to them for support, she needs to know they can handle it.

Using Facebook bypasses the safeguards

When someone makes contact through Facebook, it bypasses all the safeguards put in place to manage the exchange of information and contact. By its very nature, it enables speedy responses, and can take away the chance for people to take time to think things through. As a result, it can create tricky or even dangerous situations that can put the person in a vulnerable and difficult position. It takes away their right to say, via a third party, that they do not want any contact, or that they do not want it at this particular time. If they don't want contact, having been approached via Facebook puts them in the difficult position of having to reject the person directly (or not responding at all).

Reunion is best taken slowly, one step at a time. And preferably not via Facebook.

3 Birth relatives

These days, most adopters have a one-off meeting with their child's birth parent or parents, which often helps with subsequent letterbox contact. For many, this meeting helps them to see the child's birth parents as "sad" rather than "bad". However, many adoptive parents have never met their child's birth parents. And if their child was removed from the birth family because of abuse, they may dread the thought of them re-entering the child's life at any time. Some birth parents, over the years, manage to establish more stable, safer lives. They may mature and develop self-awareness, may have recovered from mental illness or drug and alcohol misuse and have left violent relationships. Many birth parents accept that it is best for their children to remain settled with their adoptive families. Most don't want their children's lives to be disrupted, to have them dropping out of school or running away from home. Even if they accept no responsibility for the circumstances that led to the adoption and have a burning conviction that they were the victims of injustice at the hands of social services, they may realise that it is important for the children to remain with the adoptive parents.

But a minority of birth parents live for the day when they can "get their children back". If they can find a way to trace them or get a message to them, they will. And if they can entice them back, they will.

Professor Gillian Schofield of the Centre for Research on the Child and Family, University of East Anglia, has researched the experiences of birth parents whose children have been removed by the local authority. Thirty-two parents were interviewed and at the time, most of the children were still in foster care; 18 per cent had been adopted. Some of her findings are also relevant to birth parents whose children have been adopted. She comments:

> *Parents' sense of responsibility or blame for the children coming into care varied – as did their levels of anger and subsequent sense of whether it had been overall a good thing for the children. This led to some very different pathways across the dimensions of acceptance, responsibility, blame and anger. For example:*
>
> - *Parents who accepted their responsibility and the child's need for care at the time and since, appreciating what foster care had done for the children and valuing social work support.*

- *Parents who were* angry *with professionals at the time but now accept* some responsibility *for the problems and see the benefit of care.*

- *Parents who remembered* accepting *the need for care at the time, but now talk more critically of having needed more support and think the children should have come home after the crisis was over.*

- *Parents who* blamed *and in some cases were* angry with the child *for being difficult to be cared for and therefore needing to be in care.*

- *Parents who were* angry *at the time,* blamed *social workers, did* not accept *the child's need for care and have not changed since – often becoming more angry, using years of "evidence" to support their "case", and often being* dismissive *of foster carers and the role they played in their children's lives.*

Another difference that was apparent was...

Some parents were stuck rigidly in feelings they could not resolve or move on from, particularly feelings of anger or grief. Other parents showed a remarkable ability, given their difficult circumstances, to reflect on their own experiences and empathically on the experiences of their children.

SCHOFIELD, 2009

Requests from birth relatives through the agency

Birth family members' wishes about contact may change over time – for instance, they might not have wanted contact at the time of the adoption, but they may come to feel that they would like to have some contact.

The correct way to go about this is to discuss it with the placing local authority or agency. If they have a request, e.g. to be able to send their child a birthday card, they should ask for this request to be passed on to the adoptive parents. The adoptive parents can decide whether or not to agree to it.

One day, perhaps when your child is an adult, he might decide to read all the notes from his adoption file, including your letters and comments. You don't know what will be going through his head years from now. At that particular time, he may be more inclined than you to see things from the birth parents' perspective. As a teenager or adult, he may find it difficult to understand why you made the decisions you did in response to a request that, to him, may not seem unreasonable. He may even be moved by the fact that his birth parents wanted to have contact.

It is a good idea to keep this in mind when you are deciding whether or not to agree to requests from birth relatives. If you decide to refuse a particular request, you may want to write down your reasons so that your child will have an explanation of why you made those decisions at that time.

Birth parents posting information on the internet

Birth parents' expressions of loss and grief can be heart-rending and disturbing for adoptive parents.

CASE STUDY

My husband and I adopted a little boy last April and it was made official this past December. The contact agreed with our son's (M) biological parents is one letter a year only. Out of curiosity, last year my husband and I searched for our son's parents on Facebook and they were both members. The birth mother's profile picture was in fact a close-up photograph of M sat on her knee. She had also written personal comments about M and how she regretted what had happened/will never forget him. We thought the issue was raw with her and she would eventually change her pic/stop the comments. Now we have formally adopted M but she still has the same photograph of him as her profile pic and often mentions him (as does her mother on her site), making comments such as she will never forget him and will come for him when he is 18 and that she regrets this mistake enormously.

Despite the very serious injuries her and/or her partner caused M, I have always felt empathy with this very young woman, abused herself, in and out of care and not having ever had a chance. We met them both once and they were very juvenile, I felt I was stealing M from her at the time and her Facebook page now haunts me and makes me feel the same way.

I can understand that she still feels raw about the adoption but he is no longer legally her son and we are uncomfortable with the photo on her site, her comments about him AND that she will be accessibly there as soon as M can type "Facebook". We feel we cannot force the issue for her to take off the photograph as this could make her go underground and underhand and perhaps do something in retaliation that could hurt M emotionally. It is a very tricky situation to know how to deal with.

An adoptive mother

There have been many cases in which birth parents have displayed photographs of their children on their Facebook profiles. Sometimes these photographs were taken before the adoption; sometimes they have been supplied as part of letterbox contact. (See *Birth relatives and Facebook photos*, p. 62.)

What would your child find if they "Googled" their birth name?

- A mother whose daughter was adopted as a baby posted the child's name and a message for her on a site intended for posting tributes to children who have died and condolences to their bereaved parents. At any time, if the girl "Googled" her birth name, she would find herself there, along with her birth parents' details.

- Some birth parents try to trace their children by posting messages for them on "missing people" websites and asking them to respond.

- There have been cases in which birth parents have posted the child's picture on a website or on their Facebook page, asking "Have you seen this child?" - the implication being that the child has been abducted.

Hate campaigns against social workers

Some birth parents use the internet to campaign against what they perceive as the injustice of having their children removed by children's services - one birth mother set up an online petition for her child to be returned to her. Social workers who take children into care sometimes find themselves the victims of online hate campaigns by the children's angry families.

> *A proliferation of blogs and pages on social networking sites have sprung up...social workers and managers are named and vilified, accusations are hurled at councils, and court injunctions banning the identification of the families and children are flouted...*

> *Some of the blogs are hosted in the US, where the Constitution's first amendment, guaranteeing the right to free speech, makes them all but untouchable...*

> *Myths about social services – that they get financial rewards for every adopted child or that they are involved in conspiracies to remove families' children – are perpetuated.*

> WILLIAMS, 2010

What is on the birth relatives' Facebook pages?

In a few cases, if a child searches for a birth parent or other relative, he could find content on the relative's Facebook page that could upset and/or disturb him: for example, there might be photographs of his parent drunk, or pregnant, or with another child, or pictured in provocative poses, and sexually explicit or otherwise offensive comments.

When birth relatives make contact

Facebook has only been around in the UK since 2006. Until recently, when contact arrangements were discussed pre-adoption, no one considered the possibility of birth parents ever being able to trace their children and contact them directly.

Most birth parents who try or succeed in getting in touch with an adopted child directly via internet search/social networking do not have malicious intentions, even if they realise that they shouldn't be doing it. (Of course, the contact can still be damaging for the child even if the intention is not malicious.)

- They may be anxious about the child and seeking reassurance that he is alive and well and happy.

- They may not know how to go through the proper channels to request information.

- They may feel frustrated and starved of information if adoptive parents have not kept up letterbox contact as agreed.

- They may simply fail to consider the possible impact on their child, assuming that he will be delighted to hear from them.

Going through Facebook is easy, instant and doesn't involve having to talk to a social worker. It can lead to unintended consequences for the person who initiates the contact or the one on the receiving end, or – more likely – both.

> *I really don't think there is any way of preventing this sort of thing, in all honesty. We have always been open with our daughter and talked about her past. She has never shown any interest in her birth family at all and never wanted to contribute to the contact letters we send to birth mum, which made this more of a shock. She was eight when taken into care, so knows only too well what her birth father was like. The birth parents are well aware that they are not supposed to have contact until she is 18 but that didn't stop them replying, exchanging emails and texts.*
>
> *We are reasonably confident unofficial contact has stopped – but again, there is absolutely no way of knowing for definite. It is so easy for a 16-year-old to access email on friends' laptops, at school, etc, and to set up new email accounts.*
>
> AN ADOPTIVE MOTHER

Even birth relatives who are allowed some indirect contact may try to find a way of having unmediated, direct contact:

A birth father wrote a letter to his child in which he said that he had opened a Facebook account. The adoptive parents did not pass on the letter. They wrote back to the father, pointing out that contact through social networking sites was not in the contact agreement and was not acceptable.

AN ADOPTION SOCIAL WORKER

If things like this happen, it is important to bring them to the attention of the social worker. The social worker can discuss it with the birth parents and give them advice about what is acceptable contact and also the potential negative impact of their actions.

Birth parents' use of social networking sites to make direct contact is a serious and growing problem. Adoption practice certainly needs to change to reflect this. Adoption professionals need to do more work with birth parents around the time of the adoption to help them to:

- understand the contact agreement, if there is one;
- understand the advantages and disadvantages of direct contact in adoption;
- know what they can do if their wish to establish contact becomes a pressing issue;
- understand and prioritise their child's need for stability in the placement;
- understand the potential for destabilising and possibly even serious consequences for their child if there was direct, unmediated contact through a social networking site.

I just can't bear it that birth parents don't get help or guidance to put their children first and at least try to give them the things they need, either resolution or forgiveness or just NO contact if that is what is best for the children.

AN ADOPTIVE PARENT

Establishing paternity can also be an issue. In some cases, the man named by a child's birth mother as the father is not in fact the father.

The man who had been named as the birth father of an adopted girl was putting photographs on the internet and asking for contact. We said 'Before we embark on this, we want a DNA test to be carried out.' The test showed he was not the father. The birth mother can't say who is.

AN ADOPTION SOCIAL WORKER

When children and young people trace their birth relatives

When a young person traces his birth parents or other relatives through a social networking site and makes contact, this can come as a shock to the birth parents as well as the adoptive parents. Birth parents may not have expected to hear from the child until he was at least 18. Should they respond or not? They may have been feeling bereft for a long time. They may have been thinking about their child ever since the adoption and wondering if they will ever see them again. Many are happy to hear from their child and respond immediately. Some may not be interested and don't want to know. Others may realise that this kind of contact might not be in the child's or their best interests.

CASE STUDY

A birth mother was contacted on Facebook by her daughter, aged 12. At the time of the adoption the mother had not wanted any contact and there had not been any. The birth mother contacted her local authority adoption team to let them know this had happened. She said she didn't think it would be good for the child to have contact like this and that she wanted the adoptive parents to be told. The social worker contacted the adoptive parents, who were stunned to hear what had happened. They were able to talk things over with their daughter and explain that her birth mother wanted her to wait until she was older.

As an adoptive parent, you may well be angry and unhappy if you find out that the birth parent has responded to an approach from your child. In this situation, careful thought is needed to try to identify the most helpful solution.

From the birth parents' point of view, it is unlikely that they have been given any advice, guidance or support on how they should respond to an approach from their child via a social networking site. It's entirely understandable if they don't want to ignore the child's request. But some birth parents may well understand just what a difficult situation unexpected and unmediated contact creates.

> *It was a shock. I have been worrying about her parents. They are fantastic people. I really feel for them.*
>
> A BIRTH FATHER WHOSE DAUGHTER RECENTLY MADE CONTACT WITH HER BIRTH FAMILY

Possible risks to birth parents when a child contacts them

For some birth parents, the prospect of unmediated contact is also worrying.

> *I have worked with a birth mother who has gone on to have other children, who is concerned that her eldest adopted daughter might find*

her other children on Facebook and we have talked this through and she is taking whatever measures she can to monitor this.

A POST-ADOPTION WORKER

In some cases, unexpected contact could put the birth parent at risk.

- A birth parent could be at risk from a teenager who is angry about past abuse or neglect.

- Birth relatives may be emotionally fragile or have mental health problems or learning difficulties, for example, and an unexpected approach from their adopted child could be destabilising for them.

- A birth parent may be ill or experiencing a crisis in their life.

- The birth of their child and the adoption may have been a traumatic time in their life, for instance, if the child was conceived as the result of rape. An unexpected approach from the child may stir up painful memories and difficult emotions.

- Some birth mothers belong to a family or community where sex outside marriage is taboo. Such women may have kept the pregnancy and birth and subsequent adoption a secret from other people in the extended family or community for fear of being punished or ostracised. If the child turns up in her life years later, the consequences for the woman could be serious.

- If the birth parents are no longer together, they may not have told their new partners and/or subsequent children about the child who was adopted. A young person making contact could have a destabilising impact on the parent and their family.

Young people and the internet

Few of us can now imagine life without the internet. Today's children and young people have grown up with the internet. Whether they are chatting online, organising their social lives, shopping, finding information, researching for school homework or study, downloading music, showcasing their own creativity or playing games, they get a lot out of it. We shouldn't deny any child the opportunity to use the internet responsibly and constructively.

There's no way the genie is going back in the bottle. But alongside this, children need to be well versed in the risks and dangers of the internet. This may come from parents and other adults in their lives; it is very likely to come from friends. Children who have stable lives and access to well-informed and supportive adults and friends should be able to negotiate the risks and dangers. But children who are vulnerable, feel isolated and have difficult issues in their lives may well lack basic information and support. Even if they do have it, they may, out of impulsivity, anger or a deep longing to find answers to their questions, put themselves or others at risk. It is a recipe for getting into trouble on the internet.

Parenting a young person who is tech-savvy yet emotionally ill-equipped to predict or deal with the consequences of what they do online can make for a white-knuckle ride for parents.

Vulnerable young people and online behaviour

Adopted children and teenagers may be more vulnerable than their peers online. This applies both to the general risks, which apply to any of us and our children, and to the more specific risks of searching for or communicating with birth relatives online.

Many adopted children have long-lasting vulnerabilities, however significant a recovery they may have made since being placed in their adoptive homes. These could mean that, for instance:

- they may be suggestible and easily led (e.g. by a paedophile posing as a young person in an internet chat-room or by a manipulative birth relative);

- they may not recognise risk or may actively seek out risky situations;

- they may be easily deceived;

- they may be over-confident and believe they are invulnerable;

- they may be impatient and impulsive;

- if they tend to get into arguments and fights in the real world, this can escalate online and vice versa;

- if they are victims of bullying in the real world, they may be vulnerable to cyberbullying too;

- because of their early experiences, some young people may be drawn to seeking out disturbing or otherwise unsuitable content on the internet and engage in risky and sexually harmful behaviour online;

- they may express their anger, pain and frustration online in harmful or inappropriate ways;

- those who have not developed a strong attachment to their adoptive parents are even less likely than other young people to seek their parents' advice or tell them when they are getting out of their depth;

- while searching online for birth relatives, for example, for people with a particular surname, they may make online contact with strangers who could use this as an opportunity to dupe and exploit them;

- arranging secret meetings with people (including birth relatives) they have met online could involve travelling to an unfamiliar area, alone, and could put them at risk of physical as well as emotional harm.

> *Cyberspace is a haven for adopted people because they can reinvent themselves all over again. They may have a difficult time knowing who they are, having lived without any genetic validation for so many years, and they can now become whoever they want to become via the internet. They don't seem to understand that the people with whom they are chatting are also reinventing themselves. There is a lot of lying going on on the internet.*

VERRIER, 2010

(For more information on internet safety for all age groups, see the list of organisations in *Finding out more*.)

Social use of the internet: a beginner's guide

Social use of the internet refers to the way people use the internet to interact with other people: posting messages, swapping jokes and tips, asking for or giving information or support to others, finding new and old friends, having online conversations and relationships, sharing photographs, videos, music, opinions and much more.

> *Seventy-six per cent of young people say the internet means their friends are there whenever they need them.*

THE FUTURES COMPANY/YOUTHNET, 2009

Many mobile phones are now internet-enabled – so in order to access the internet and use many of the applications below, often the only technology needed is a mobile phone.

If you don't know the first thing about the internet, here is a brief introduction.

Search engines

Google is the most widely-used search engine. Simply typing in someone's name into Google (www.google.com) or another search engine reveals links to any information about them on websites across the whole of the internet. In some cases this will include certain information from social networking sites such as Facebook. The search engine may lead you to their Facebook profile but you may not be able to see all the personal information on their profile (see Chapter 5).

Instant messaging

Instant messaging (IM) allows friends who have exchanged their email addresses to send messages to each other in real time, when they are online at the same time. This is done through instant-messaging services provided by internet service providers (e.g. AOL Instant Messenger, Windows Live Messenger). You can also instant-message via social networking sites such as Facebook and many other websites. If users have a webcam (a camera incorporated in or attached to their computer) they can see each other as well as read messages from each other.

You can also send and receive instant messages from most mobile phones (see below).

Internet chatrooms

Chatrooms allow several users who are online at the same time to exchange instant messages with each other. People don't identify themselves – they use a "username" instead. The nature of this kind of communication can disinhibit people and lead them to do and say things that they wouldn't do in "real life". There have also been a number of cases in which paedophiles have targeted young people in chatrooms by pretending to be another young person.

Games consoles

Games consoles such as Nintendo DS, Sony Playstation 3 and Nintendo Wii can be used to access the internet; your child may be playing computer games but he could also be instant-messaging people at the same time. You may want to think about setting parental controls for games consoles as well as computers.

Skype

This is an application which allows people to speak to each other over the internet free of charge. It means you can have a "proper" conversation without big phone bills. With a webcam you can see each other as well. Skype can be great if, for instance, you want your adopted child to be able to keep in touch with birth brothers and sisters or other relatives elsewhere in the UK or even another country.

Tracing and reunion websites

The internet is home to a huge number of "where are you now?" and "missing people" sites as well as organisations (commercial and non-profit) that offer to help you trace people you've lost touch with or research your family tree. Some websites have **discussion boards** or **message boards** on which people can leave messages for people they want to make contact with.

The Missing You website (www.missing-you.net) has literally thousands of messages posted by people who are searching for someone. There is an adoption section which lists messages from adult adoptees searching for birth relatives or from birth relatives looking for family members adopted many years earlier. In one or two of the messages, birth mothers address their young children who are living with adoptive families.

On the Genes Reunited site (www.genesreunited.co.uk), people can register in the hope of getting in touch with relatives – with obvious appeal for some adopted children wanting to find out about their origins, as well as birth relatives hoping to trace children.

Websites and groups for birth parents

There are a number of websites for "self-help" organisations for people whose children have gone through or are going through care proceedings, or whose children have been adopted. There are Facebook groups for people interesting in tracing family members (e.g. Familylink) and groups started by parents who are aggrieved that their children have been removed by children's services.

Bebo

Bebo is an acronym for Blog Early, Blog Often. It is a social networking site which was founded in January 2005. The company itself describes the site as providing 'an open, engaging and fun environment that empowers a new generation to discover, connect and express themselves'. Bebo is similar to other social networking sites, offering the user the chance to set up a profile, which includes a comments section for messages, and a list of the user's friends. Many more modules can be added, as can photos and videos; it also offers the opportunity to join various groups and link the Bebo profile to other services. Three privacy levels are offered: public, private and fully private. Public profiles can be seen by anyone except that profiles of users younger than 16 are seen only by logged-in users; private profiles can only be seen by friends and members of any group the user has joined; while fully private profiles are ones where the user has not joined any group, so only their direct friends can view the profile.

YouTube

This is a site on which people can post videos so that other people can access them via the internet. For instance, an aspiring band might put a video of themselves on YouTube. In some cases, people recommend a video clip to their friends, who recommend it to their friends and it ends up "going viral" and being seen by thousands or millions of people around the world. YouTube can also be used in a sinister way – there have been many cases of assaults and bullying being recorded on mobile phones and posted on the internet for others to view.

Flickr

This is a photo-sharing website.

Blogs

Blogs are websites – weblogs – with regularly updated content. If you write a blog, you write regular instalments rather like a diary and post them on the internet for others to read.

Twitter

"Tweeting" is like blogging (above) but the messages are very short. People subscribe to another person's (or organisation's) Twitter feed, which means they receive Twitter messages ("tweets") whenever that person or organisation sends them out. Tweets can be sent and received via email and mobile phone.

Mobile phones

- Many mobile phones can also be used to access the internet. So if you have set up filtering or monitoring on your home computer to prevent access to unsuitable websites, remember that you may need to set up similar features on your child's phone too.

- Some people use their mobile phones to take photographs of themselves (or someone else) naked or in suggestive poses and then send the pictures, by phone, to someone else's phone ("sexting"). Sometimes girls are persuaded or bullied into doing this by boyfriends or men they have befriended online. Of course, these photographs can subsequently be circulated around any number of other people or be posted on the internet where they may end up being seen by thousands.

> *Birth parents once tried to slip the child their mobile phone number during contact to ask him to keep in touch and have tried to give him a gift of a mobile so they could keep in touch with him.*
>
> AN ADOPTION SOCIAL WORKER

Location services on mobile phones

Location services, which can identify your location via your mobile phone, are becoming popular. A guide for parents from Vodafone explains the implications:

> *Until recently, the focus of location-based services was on personal location and navigation with the user asking the question 'Where am I?' Now, the focus is moving towards more social 'Where are you?' and 'Here I am!' services, where users opt into services within a mapping or social networking application.*
>
> HTTP://PARENTS.VODAFONE.COM/LOCATIONSERVICES

For instance, there are applications such as Google Latitude which let you share your location with your friends and family when you are out and about. A young person can sign up to use this kind of location service alongside their Facebook profile, so that everyone on their "friends" list can see where they are.

Location services can be abused. Think about the implications: if birth relatives are on the friends list, they would know the child's location to within a few metres and might be able to work out where they live or go to school (as these will be their most regular locations).

There are also passive location (tracking) devices that use locations provided by the mobile network.

- *Explain (to your child) that they should never accept a mobile from anyone (known or unknown to them) without your agreement, as it might be pre-installed with passive location services.*

- *If you're really worried about location-based services, don't give your child a mobile with GPS or Wi-Fi on it or, if they already have a mobile, disable GPS or Wi-Fi on their handset.*

HTTP://PARENTS.VODAFONE.COM/LOCATIONSERVICES

You and your child both need to know about the risks and understand the precautions you should take.

For more information, read parents' guides to mobile location services, such as those produced by Vodafone and Ofcom (see *Finding out more*).

Online communication: some of the risks

Because of the developments in social media, some of which are listed above, children and young people can potentially "meet" online, not just birth relatives but a wide range of people from around the world whom they would never normally come into contact with.

In cyberspace there are well-documented risks which apply to all of us, such as:

- internet fraud;
- identity theft;
- hackers hacking into accounts to steal passwords and access bank details, etc;
- "phishing" - fraudulent emails that trick people into giving away personal details;
- online bullying, harassment or abuse or other unwanted approaches (either from known people or strangers);
- approaches from paedophiles grooming children for sexual purposes;

- coming across (or searching for) content of a violent, pornographic or horrific nature;
- sites which could be harmful to vulnerable people, such as those which discuss self-harm or anorexia (in inappropriate ways) or suicide sites.

For more information: there's a huge amount of advice out there about how to avoid the risks (see *Finding out more*).

All children and young people need to understand *and put into practice* common-sense measures such as:

- never giving out personal details online;
- never meeting anyone in real life whom they have only met on the internet;
- knowing what to do about any online contact which makes them feel uncomfortable.

These measures, of course, should apply to communication with birth relatives just as much as strangers. Many of the usual precautions to keep children safe on the internet will – to a certain extent - protect them from being traced or contacted by birth relatives. But adoptive families and adopted children and young people need to take extra precautions, which are covered in Chapters 6 and 7 of this book.

Oversharing

Online communication is very different from face-to-face communication and people use it differently. People sometimes behave online in ways that they wouldn't in the real world. Some forms of communication, such as instant messaging with one other person, can feel very private and intimate. People may write things which they might not express face to face. They can be put off their guard and may be drawn into revealing information that they shouldn't. Teenagers often share personal information about themselves and others with their friends, social networking contacts and even the wider web as a whole, in a way that many adults would find inappropriate or even shocking. They bare their emotions and write about their thoughts, experiences and relationships with little thought for how they might be laying themselves open. They may be less inhibited. They may be rude or aggressive online in a way that they wouldn't be, face to face.

We have a 16-year-old girl on a Special Guardianship Order. She was given information about her 18-year-old sister and went straight on Facebook to find her. In our case this isn't a problem except that our daughter's behaviour on Facebook is now fed directly into her family who will be horrified to see how she behaves with her friends. She has an overpowering relationship with her boyfriend and there are countless aggressive arguments between them and friends on various pages. She has even had semi-nude photos of herself posted. The police have been to print off one conversation because the content led to the boyfriend's mother's car being damaged.

She has all our relatives on her "friends" list and they can all see what happens and tell us they are concerned for her.

A SPECIAL GUARDIAN

Obsessive use of the internet

The internet is in your home – it's always there, it's always on. Many young people spend hours on the computer each night, chatting and catching up with what their friends are doing. Some parents feel that their teenagers' Facebook use is obsessive and they find it difficult or impossible to control. Checking for new emails and using Facebook can become compulsive, particularly if you are desperately waiting for a reply or you have a special reason to be interested in someone.

This young woman came across her half-sister and birth father on Facebook:

I have turned into an online stalker. That first accidental glimpse has turned into a low-level obsession. I check Lee-Anne's Facebook page every day. I have followed a link to a video blog that my father updates regularly with clips of himself doing karaoke and telling jokes. I now know where he lives, works and drinks, all information I never had before and all just from looking at web pages...I am fascinated by these people even though I know that what I'm doing is borderline odd. I don't want to meet a man who is only biologically my father, but I can't stop watching him either. I like the fact that I know more about him than he knows about me. I can satisfy my curiosity, without the fear that he will reject me. Nothing has actually changed in my life – and yet everything is different somehow.

I HAVE NEVER MET MY BIRTH FATHER BUT NOW I AM FOLLOWING HIS EVERY MOVE ON FACEBOOK, AN ACCOUNT PUBLISHED IN *THE GUARDIAN*, 30.07.09.

On Facebook, you can do the following

Social networking sites such as Facebook, Bebo and MySpace allow users to link and interact with others online.

Facebook has by far the largest number of users – in just four years, from 2006 to 2010, it has attracted over 23 million users in the UK. It is the site that is involved in the vast majority of cases of adopted children tracing birth relatives. With Facebook, you can search for a person by name – you don't need to know their email address, which is the case with some other social networking sites.

- Set up a "personal profile" – a "page" of your own on the internet, with a profile photograph of yourself, on which you can write about yourself and your likes and dislikes and display all of this to other people.

- Update it as often as you like, writing messages about what you've been doing or thinking about.

- Include links on your page to other websites that you like, e.g. charities you support or video clips or a blog.

- Link to your friends' profiles and, through them, see some of their friends' profiles.

- Send a request to other people (e.g. people you have met in the real world), asking to become their "friend" on the social networking site.

- Become a "friend" of your friends' friends or indeed anyone on Facebook (if they accept your request).

- Post "albums" of your photographs on your page, which you can choose to make available for your friends and other people to see.

- "Instant message" your friends via the site if they are online at the same time as you.

- Read what your friends have posted on your "wall" – you and your friends can post comments, questions, jokes, and reminders for each other.

- Use the site as a one-stop social calendar to manage your social life, suggest get-togethers, invite your friends to parties and other events, and so on.

- Send online friends "gifts" (an icon or picture of something, like a birthday cake on their birthday) or a "poke" to say 'I'm thinking about you'.

- Join "groups" on Facebook to show that you like the same things, support the same causes or just agree with a particular statement (which may be serious or humorous).

The appeal of Facebook and other social networking sites is clear. It's about your identity – who you are, what you are into – and friendship. Some young people accept "friends requests" from anyone and end up with literally hundreds of "friends". For some, the number of online "friends" they have feels like a measure of their popularity.

Part of the appeal is that a social networking site feels like an adult-free zone where they can express themselves however they want.

However, some young people may misunderstand the nature of social networking.

> *Many users believe they are writing for a closed group of friends, unaware that the information they have posted may be publicly available and able to be searched for and read by a much wider audience.*

CHILDNET REPORT

Social networking sites such as Facebook are 'more important than family' to a quarter of children, according to a survey commissioned in 2010 by National Family Week. The study surveyed 1,000 children from eight to 15 across the UK. Twenty-eight per cent of children questioned cited websites such as Facebook, Twitter and MSN as the most important thing to them. For girls, the top three choices were popularity and having friends, followed by family and then social networking sites (chosen by four in 10 girls). Fewer boys chose social networking – their top three were family, money and then popularity and friends.

Online safety and your child's privacy

Parental controls and monitoring tools

Parental controls can help keep children safe online. They can prevent children from seeing harmful and inappropriate content online and monitor their behaviour. But children and young people also need to know about how to keep themselves safe.

Using certain online security software (free or paid for), you can, for instance:

- filter out websites not suitable for children, by age range or category;

- stop children viewing specific inappropriate websites;

- set different ratings for web content for different members of the family, e.g. one for your nine-year-old and one for your 15-year-old;

- set time limits for how long your children can spend online or block access at specific times of day;

- get email or text alerts when your child attempts to access a blocked website or when he posts any confidential information.

Fifty three per cent of parents of eight- to 11-year-olds use parental control software.

OFCOM MEDIA LITERACY AUDIT, 2009

There are monitoring tools which inform adults about a child's online activity without necessarily limiting access. Some of these tools simply record the addresses of websites that a child has visited. Others provide a warning message to a child if he visits an inappropriate site. Monitoring tools can be used with or without the knowledge of the child. Explaining all these and how they work is beyond the scope of this book. But there is plenty of information available online through your internet service provider and other organisations. Or you can ask knowledgeable sales assistants in computer shops. If you are not especially IT-literate (and you don't have a willing friend who can help), you just have to grit your teeth and make the effort to read and find out about it.

Bear in mind that some young people are skilled in finding ways of getting around filters and controls. And if your child wants to be found, or is actively looking for birth parents, these measures won't stop him (though they will protect him from other dangers). Even if you install parental controls and tight security settings on your home computer, your child may still access the internet through friends' computers or computers at school or in a library or an internet café. And perhaps his mobile phone...

Remember: the best internet security in the world is no substitute for talking to your child about his adoption and his birth family.

Knowing more about what your child does online might alert you to the fact that he is curious and is searching for information. It could be a wake-up call to let you know you might need to bring up the subject of his adoption and his birth parents. If he'll talk to you about this, you have the chance of helping and supporting him with what he needs to know, as explained in Chapters 1 and 2 of this book.

Don't appear anti-internet!

The more you know about the internet, the better. Your child is less likely to listen to what you say about the internet if you give the impression that you think it's all bad. He'll also resent it if you don't give him some credit for being sensible online.

A group of adopted young people were asked "What do you want your adoptive parent to know about the internet and your use of it?" Some of their replies were:

- *I am not stupid so you need to trust me.*
- *I know ways of keeping myself safe on the internet and I can show you.*
- *Don't knock it till you try it.*
- *It's not all about porn!*
- *If it wasn't the internet you would only worry about something else.*

Checking which websites have been visited

You may wonder whether your child has been visiting sites such as Genes Reunited or Facebook. Searching the browser "history" will give you a list of websites that have been visited.

Internet Explorer is the browser most often used in the UK. On Internet Explorer, click on the "Favourites" button on the toolbar (the one you use to save your favourite webpages). This will bring up three tabs: "Favourites", "Feeds" and "History". Click on "History" and you will be able to view a list of the web pages that have been visited. You can sort these either alphabetically or by date visited, or by most visited.

Remember:

- It's easy to delete the history, so if your child is attempting to cover his tracks by deleting it, you won't be able to check which websites he has been looking at. He may have deleted the history because he's been looking at other "unsuitable" websites he doesn't want you to know about. But knowing that he is trying to hide something from you is a start!
- If you don't find a particular site listed in the history, you can't be sure he isn't visiting that site on a different computer (or via a different browser on your computer).

- There may be more than one browser on your computer, so you would need to check the history of each browser. It's possible for a young person to install an alternative browser on the computer (e.g. Mozilla Firefox, Safari) either intentionally or unintentionally (e.g. when they use certain applications such as i-Tunes).

If you want to hide your visits to certain websites...

If you don't want your child or young person to see which sites on the internet you have visited, don't forget to clear this data. (For instance, in Internet Explorer, go to "Safety" and click on "Delete browsing history".)

How far should you go?

Internet safety organisations recommend that parents and other adults discuss and explain the use of monitoring tools with children so that they can learn appropriate behaviour on the internet.

If you are concerned that your child may be at risk, you could decide to log or monitor his conversations, and this can be done through some forms of filtering software – but think carefully about the implications of this. If you tell your child you are monitoring things, he may feel that you don't trust him and he may start hiding more from you. If you don't tell him, you have to consider the message that it would send to him if he found out. How would he react? He might be extremely angry about it, and end up being more secretive and less willing to share things with you. Also, if you found out something this way, how would you deal with it? If he realises how you have found out, he may not be in the right frame of mind when you try to sit down and talk to him about what is on his mind. He would probably try to deflect it by going on the attack and making it all about you "spying" on him.

As a parent, you have to decide what action you feel is justified, given the circumstances and the level of risk, and what is the best approach to use with your child, given his age and personality. Is it possible to tell him that you are keeping an eye on things he does online and explain why? You can be matter-of-fact about it and say that it is your job as a parent to keep him safe.

It is our responsibility to protect our children and we shouldn't be defensive about this. We should not be afraid of setting rules for our children's internet use or apologetic about this. Obviously, the child's age and track record are important here. With younger children, it is often easier to identify acceptable boundaries. With teenagers, there are shades of grey as you allow them more freedom and they become more resistant to what they see as attempts to "control" what they do. Children and teenagers are entitled to a level of privacy. Is it ever right to read a teenager's diary, for instance? Probably you would do this only if you had good reason to believe he was in some serious trouble or danger. As the parent, it's your call and you have to decide what action you feel is justified, given the circumstances and the level of risk.

Can you be your child's Facebook friend?

If you are on Facebook yourself and your child will let you become his "friend", you will be able to keep an eye on his activities, who his friends are and so on.

It sometimes seems that adults and children are each trying to keep one step ahead of the other...

> *He doesn't realise that I can see what he's doing and thinks he can tell me he's not on his laptop but he is...I know he is because he's on Facebook and then he gets caught out and I tell him to go to bed through Facebook!*
>
> A GRANDMOTHER OF TWO, QUOTED IN UK COUNCIL FOR CHILD INTERNET SAFETY, 2009

Some parents manage to negotiate an agreement to be able to check their child's social networking activity. (If you are allowed access, be prepared to be surprised by some of the things your child and his friends share and the language they use...and don't ruin things by writing embarrassing messages on his wall!)

But of course, some young people would do anything rather than let their parents access their Facebook page.

Some parents may try to find solutions such as:

- tightening up their child's Facebook privacy settings (you can only do this if you know his password or if he leaves the computer while still logged in to his account);

- setting up a Facebook account under a false name so they can become his "friend" if he accepts the request (using a false name is against Facebook's rules, by the way). But see below, *Can adults contact children via Facebook?* Think carefully about the implications about this - it is a form of deception and could impact badly on your relationship with your child.

> *An adoptive mother who monitors her child's Facebook account sees that a birth sibling has sent a request to become the child's friend. She deletes it. It happens again. She continues to delete the requests but knows it is only a matter of time...*

We should always ask ourselves: what are we trying to protect children from? Secret monitoring, banning and blocking are unlikely to be the best ways to offer this protection.

Things are changing all the time...

> *We don't yet know the full consequences for a generation that has grown up online, or the future implications of new types of search, for*

example, social searches, which aggregate information from across a range of social networking sites by your name or email address, or of the development of facial-recognition search software.

CHILDNET REPORT

Using privacy settings is vital

Using the Facebook privacy settings, you can limit the ability to view your profile and certain items on a Facebook page to certain categories of people, e.g.:

- friends;
- friends of friends;
- everyone;
- or you can customise it to include or exclude ("block") individual people.

Thirty-one per cent of 12- to15-year-olds don't use privacy settings on their social networking profiles

OFCOM MEDIA LITERACY AUDIT, 2009

In terms of how publicly available Facebook information is, the situation is changing all the time. Facebook has taken steps towards opening up parts of its site to internet search engines such as Google, a move which led to much confusion and protest.

The default privacy settings for certain categories of information is set to "Everyone". These changes mean that, unless you actively change your privacy settings, certain personal information is viewable by "everyone" (everyone with a Facebook account) rather than just Facebook "friends".

Until their 18th birthday, young Facebook users don't have public search listings created for them, and the visibility of their information is limited to friends of friends, and networks, even if they have chosen to make it available to everyone. However, this doesn't apply to their name, profile picture, gender and network, which are visible to everyone.

You should leave the "city" and "gender" fields blank if you do not want them seen by people.

Certain information on Facebook is already available across the wider internet. And Microsoft has announced plans to incorporate Facebook messages that are flagged for the general public into its search engine results – so sooner or later, it's likely that Facebook will become much more "searchable" across the web.

- If you post something on your Facebook page, then – depending on your settings – not only your friends but possibly also their friends or indeed everyone with a Facebook account may be able to see it. You can control exactly who sees each piece of information you post on your page - but many young people don't bother changing the default privacy settings.

- You don't have to be on it to be in it - even if you don't have a Facebook account yourself, friends or family can put photographs or videos of you (or mention you by name) on it.

- If someone is "tagged" in a photograph (which means their name is attached to it, as in a caption), "friends" of other people in the same photograph may be able to see the photograph. Facebook tells you if you have been tagged in a photograph.

- If someone writes on your wall, your friends can see what they are writing, unless you set your privacy settings high enough to prevent this.

- At the time of writing, you cannot stop "friends of friends" from asking to become your friend on Facebook (but you don't have to agree to the requests).

- Facebook also makes "friends suggestions" of its own. For instance, if A knows B, C and D, and B, C and D have a mutual friend E, it might suggest to A that they become friends with E.

- If people live and go to school or socialise in a small area and have many local "friends", it is highly likely that their "friends" will be friends with or even related to each other. So their names may pop up as "friends suggestions" for other people in the same village or area.

- "Friends" of course can sometimes change their minds about being friends. So instead of fun messages, young people can find themselves on the receiving end of abuse and bullying and worse.

Declining Facebook friend requests and removing friends

- If you want to decline a friend request or remove someone from your Facebook friend list, you can do this without attracting attention. You can decline a request by selecting "ignore". They won't be told that you have declined their request, but they will be able to send you another request in the future unless you "block" them. You will be asked, "Do you want to block this person?"

- If you take no action on the request they've sent you, they will not be able to send you another friend request. When they view you in "search" or elsewhere on Facebook, you will appear as a pending friend request until you either accept or ignore the request.

- You can remove people as friends by scrolling down to the bottom left side of their Facebook profiles and selecting the link "Remove from Friends". The person will not be notified, but they will be removed from your Friend list and you will be removed from theirs.

Illustrations of how the privacy settings work are presented in the appendix.

People are not always who they say they are…

As on the rest of the internet, people on Facebook are not always who they say they are. There have been cases of "identity theft" in which people have obtained other people's photographs and set up a fake Facebook profile purporting to be that other person, complete with photograph. They can then use this fake profile to "befriend" other people, either in order to gain access to information they wouldn't otherwise be able to get, or to target them maliciously.

Can adults contact children via Facebook?

It is Facebook policy that over-18s cannot use the site to search for under-18s. Facebook says that the default privacy settings on profiles of under-18s prevent them from being contacted by over-18s unless there is already a link between them (e.g. if they share certain friends or belong to the same network).

However, it is possible for this to happen in various ways, including:

- under-18s can enter a false date of birth;
- an adult can enter a false date of birth which makes out they are under 18;
- an adult can enlist the help of another under-18 to use their account to search for and contact the child.

NB: Using a false date of birth contravenes Facebook's terms and conditions.

Controlling who sees you online

With most instant messaging services, you can choose which friends see you as online or offline by using "stealth settings". If you want to sign in but not let your friends know you're online, select the "Sign in as Invisible" option when you log in. Once you're signed in, you can see which of your friends are online but they can't see you. You can still send and receive messages, even if you appear offline. If you are already signed in and want to become invisible to your friends, change your status to "Invisible to Everyone". This will instantly make you appear offline to your friends. With some versions of instant messaging services, you can appear online to some friends but offline to others. You can access individual stealth settings by right-clicking on a friend in your contact list. You can also appear invisible to an entire group (e.g. relatives).

This means: suppose you are online using the family computer and your child is in another room. You might see that he is offline and assume he's doing his homework. But he could in fact be using the stealth settings to appear offline (invisible) to you, while instant-messaging someone else…

"Blocking" people

If you receive an instant message from someone that you do not want to be in contact with, you can click the "Ignore/Add to Ignore List" button in the instant messaging window to permanently block their messages. The person you're blocking will not know that you have chosen to ignore their messages. If your child wants to avoid people who are trying to instant-message him (e.g. birth relatives), he can "block" them so they will not be able to send him messages. You can also block individual people by name to prevent them finding you or contacting you on Facebook.

Searching for someone on Facebook

You can sometimes find someone by going to the Facebook site and searching for their name. However, if it is common, there may be lots of people listed with that name (Facebook has 400 million users worldwide).

Against some of the names there will be displayed a "profile shot", which may be a photograph the person has uploaded to their page. Some people may leave their profile shot blank or use an illustration, a general photo, a photo of their cat or their tattoo or whatever. You may recognise the person you are searching for by their photograph. Even if there are a number of people with the same name and you do not know what the person looks like, you could conceivably send messages to all of them, to find out if they are the person you are looking for.

If you can identify the right person, you can go to their Facebook page. Depending on their security settings, you may be able to see very little information about them. But if their privacy settings are set so that "everyone" can see their page, you may be able to find out quite a lot about them. You can also see people's "friends", often with their photographs as well, and click through to their pages.

If you want to contact a person through Facebook, you can sign up to Facebook yourself and send a request to become that person's "friend" and, if you like, send them a message at the same time. If they accept your request to be their friend, you can then see everything on their page that they have set to the level of "friends". For instance, you will probably be able to read messages on their "wall" between them and their friends, see their photo albums, find out a lot more about them and their interests and the places they go to, as well as being able to send more messages to them via Facebook. With this level of access it can be quite easy to find out which school or college a child or young person goes to, or even perhaps where they are meeting their friends that evening. If you are in a person's "friends" list and you are both online at the same time, you can send an instant message to the person.

Think of the implications of this: suppose your child has a Facebook page and has unwittingly accepted a birth brother or sister as a friend. He could be using his computer one evening and up pops an instant message from a birth brother or sister – they are online and waiting for an immediate response. This is why adopted children and young people should never accept friend requests from people they do not know personally.

There are various tools you can use to:

- hide certain items on Facebook from other people;

- create groups of friends (so you can choose to show the group and no one else);

- block certain people altogether (so that if they searched for your name it would not come up).

But remember that, if you block a birth parent by name, but they have already had contact with your child, they can easily re-establish it by:

- setting up another account in a different name and contacting him again;

- contacting him via the account of one of their friends (or another of their children);

- contacting him via the account of one of his friends (some birth parents have been known to "friend" their children's Facebook friends...).

Birth relatives: can they trace children?

Many birth parents will not want to or may not be able to find their children through social networking sites. Some actively want to do so or are simply curious. Others will be prepared to and will know how to carry out a sustained search online.

When a child is adopted, the child's new surname is meant to be kept secret. But even without the surname, it is possible to find people on the internet and on social networking sites in particular. A determined person who is prepared to put in the time can piece together bits of information they know or have gleaned and an internet search can provide leads which they may be able to follow up.

What might lead a birth parent to your family?

- Even if they don't know the child's new surname, an unusual first name could be a way of tracing him.

- They may search the internet for the child, for instance, by using the child's two first names or the first name(s) in combination with any other information they know, such as his date of birth or the city he lives in.

- If two children were adopted together, the parent could carry out a search for the two names and find instances where those two names are mentioned together.

- If the child is good at a particular sport or musical instrument, for example, they may search for and find his name in sports reports or reports of performances or awards, particularly if they know the town or city he lives in.

- If the birth parents have met the adoptive parents and know their first names – particularly if these are distinctive – they may be able to search for both the parents' names and find instances where they appear together. They may also be able to search for the parents' names on social networking sites and recognise them from their profile photographs.

- If some information has been given pre-adoption or during face-to-face contact, such as the parents' first names and occupations, the birth parents may be able to search for items on the internet that could identify the adoptive family.

- See also, *Photographs: a way of tracing a child?* (p. 64)

- If a birth parent knows the town or city where the young person lives, they could identify one or two schools he might attend. The parent could then look at the members of Facebook groups connected with these schools. If the young person has joined the group, this might be a route by which the birth parent could try to trace him.

- Remember that, in theory, a birth parent should not be able to find a child's own profile on Facebook even if they know his name – over-18s are not meant to be able to find or contact under-18s. (See *Can adults contact children via Facebook?* p. 47 (above).)

> *I think parents who use these sites need to keep in mind how easy it is to identify possible hits from very little information if you are prepared to put the time in.*

AN ADOPTIVE PARENT

The court hearing

If you have not yet adopted a child, consider having the adoption hearing held in a court in the area from which the child has been placed rather than your own area, so as not to provide information about where you live.

> *Since adopting M, both my husband and I have disconnected from our "local networking" site – so we are not identifiable to a place. We figure that even though the birth parents only know our first names (though with so many people involved in the adoption – some more professional than others - we always wonder whether our surnames are really a mystery to them), with drive and determination, they would only need to spend a couple of days looking for our first names to match our profile pics. So we also never use our own profile pics. We also make photographs of M private to our friends only.*

AN ADOPTIVE PARENT

> *There have always been concerns about keeping adopters' identities safe for the benefit of children and many occasions where a lack of care on the part of professionals has revealed their location, thereby putting children at risk. But in these cases, the risks were avoidable with more care. I'm not at all sure this is true with social networking sites without cutting families off from what is rapidly becoming a key method of keeping in touch with family and friendship groups...*

I am saddened that the careful process put in place to protect and support adoptees with tracing or being traced (including their right for a veto) seems so significantly compromised.

Social workers must ensure that they keep all adopters' information safe during the early stages of matching and beyond. A throwaway remark about an adopter's job or current location can lead to compromised security of the placement. Courts too, especially in the light of recent proposals for opening up the family courts, need to safeguard this information.

They should also be mindful of the issues when setting up direct contact and monitor letterbox carefully. Herein lies a minefield, especially where some siblings are in touch with birth family and others not.

LYNDA GILBERT, POLICY CONSULTANT TO ADOPTION UK

Should you change a child's first name?

If you have not yet adopted a child, you may be wondering whether – in the Facebook age – it is safer to change the child's first name as well as his surname to make it much harder for birth relatives to trace him. This is a difficult question and one that arouses strong feelings. Adoption preparation classes have always stressed the importance of retaining a child's first name because it is such a vital part of his identity. But now that the internet has made tracing much easier, there are situations where adopters and professionals involved in adoption are wondering whether, when the birth family poses a threat, the need to protect a child's identity outweighs the arguments in favour of keeping his name. Some adopters say they wish they had changed the child's first name. And there are examples of adopters simply going ahead and doing it as soon as they can.

Adoption agencies are starting to develop risk assessment tools to help them in weighing up levels of risk and how these may impact on contact arrangements. Changing a child's first name is a significant decision which is likely to need addressing in a minority of cases where there are significant risks posed by the birth parents or the uniqueness of a child's name. These decisions should only be taken after a full assessment of the issues. Sometimes, changing an unusual spelling to a more usual one might be all that is necessary.

It is also important to remember that in many cases of Facebook contact, it is the young person who makes the contact – not the birth parent. So unless we are prepared to keep the child's name secret from him until he is 18, there are no guarantees that even changing the name would prevent direct contact.

51

Changing his surname

There is case law which makes it clear that adopters have to continue using the child's birth family surname until the adoption order has been granted. This means that, when he is first placed with them, they have to register him in school and with a doctor in his birth surname rather than the one he is going to have. If this applies to you, take extra care during this period to keep his identity secret from the world at large. Make sure the school understands the importance of this, and that all the professionals you are dealing with understand the need for your child's electronic records to be shielded with an extra level of security. Local authorities should already be doing this.

HOW YOUNG PEOPLE CAN PROTECT THEIR PRIVACY ON SOCIAL NETWORKING SITES

- They should use the highest privacy settings so that their information can be seen only by known friends.

- They should not accept random unknown people as "friends". Doing this increases the risk that they will inadvertently accept a birth parent or sibling as a friend.

- They should not make public any information that could help someone identify them, such as their date of birth.

- If there is a risk that their birth parents know their surname, or if they have an unusual first name, they should use a nickname on Facebook instead of their real name.

- They could spell their name in a different way for their Facebook profile (e.g. Nıck Smıth).

- They must remember that a person on Facebook may be using an assumed name - they may not be who they pretend to be.

- They shouldn't use a profile photograph, if there's a risk that a birth parent or friends of the birth parents might come across it and recognise them. They could either not use a photo at all, or use one in which they are not easily identified, or use a cartoon or illustration.

- They shouldn't publicly post any information about their school or local area (or photographs with any identifying details like car registration numbers or street names).

- To prevent birth relatives or siblings contacting them on Facebook, they could block them individually by name (though this doesn't stop them opening an account in a different name or using a friend's account and contacting them that way).

- Often young people join groups or networks connected with their school or college. Obviously if your child does this, someone with access to their profile information could work out where they live and even potentially track them down in the real world.

- Even if your child doesn't include any information about their school on their own profile, their friends probably do on theirs – and anyone viewing their profile can click through to their friends' profiles to find out about them and where they go to school. It may be safer for an adopted young person to hide their list of friends (click on the pencil icon in the top right-hand corner of the "Friends" box on your profile and untick the box that says "Show my friends on my profile").

Remember that your child or teenager won't want to protect their privacy if they are actively looking for birth relatives or want to be found – some teenagers secretly sabotage efforts to keep their online identity private. And they may have more than one Facebook account.

Facebook and adoptive families

Some good news about social networking

- Post-adoption social workers can use it to trace the birth families of adoptees (of all ages) at their request, when other methods have failed.

- It can be a good way for adopted children and adoptive families to keep in touch when contact with birth siblings, parents and other relatives has been agreed – particularly if they are geographically far apart.

- Many adoptive parents have Facebook accounts of their own, either because they appreciate everything Facebook offers; because they want to understand how it works; and/or so they can keep an eye on what their child is up to and who her friends are.

Using Facebook to find your child's birth relatives

Many adoptive parents also use Facebook to search for their child's birth relatives to find out about them or find out what their child might discover if they searched for them. Depending on their privacy settings, certain information may be viewable without necessarily becoming a "friend" of the birth parent.

If you request to become a friend of a birth parent and they accept, this means they can then see all the information that you have set to the level of "friends" on your own profile. To get round this, some adoptive parents have used a pseudonym to set up a fake profile in order to send a "friend request" to their child's birth parent or other relatives. If accepted, this allows them to access information open to the birth parent's "friends", without compromising their own privacy in the process. Registering an account under a false name is against Facebook rules (although many people do use nicknames). Some adoptive parents feel this is also unethical, while others believe it is justified in the interests of their child. If you decide to go down this route, you need to consider how you would explain your actions to your child later on and the possible implications for any positive contact with birth family members that you might want in the future.

Some adoptive parents even print off photographs from birth parents' Facebook pages to show their children when they are older (one adoption worker had also done this).

CASE STUDY
....

I actually have a positive Facebook story to report, in that I was able to finally see a photograph of my toddler daughter's birth father – and print it off for posterity in her life story book.

My little girl's birth father had refused to co-operate with any social workers by providing pictures or personal information – and the details supplied about him by the birth mother are very sketchy, to say the least. In fact, prior to tracking him down on Facebook, I only knew, third-hand, one very random piece of information about him.

Mindful of having my online footsteps traced, I used an acquaintance's Facebook log-in to search for his extremely unusual – if not totally unique – name and came up trumps with the photo that I think will be so important to my daughter.

An adoptive parent

Parents sometimes wonder whether, if they look at the birth parent's Facebook profile, the birth parent will somehow be able to tell. You sometimes hear people say there are ways of finding out who has viewed their page. We asked Facebook: is it possible to tell who is viewing or has viewed your Facebook page (if they are not in your "friends" list)? Is there an application that will allow you to find this out? Facebook said:

> *Facebook does not provide a way for you to see who's viewing your profile, nor can applications do this. Applications that claim to be able to do this violate Facebook's Developer Principles and Policies and are quickly disabled by our enforcement team when we find them or they're reported to us by our users.*

Avoiding being traced through links

If there's a risk that there may be any Facebook links between your family and friends and any members of the birth family or their friends:

- Ask your friends and family not to "tag" their Facebook photographs with your child's name (or your own name, if you think this could lead people to your child).
- If you have been tagged in a photograph, you can use a button underneath the photograph which allows you to "de-tag" it.
- Ask other people never to use your child's name on websites, in blogs, etc.
- Get your child to tell her friends not to "tag" her in photographs.

In addition, you may want to avoid any photographs of your child appearing anywhere on the internet.

CASE STUDY

An adopted young person aged 14 found her birth family via Facebook. She had not disclosed her new name but she had given her mobile phone number. The adopters contacted the social worker who had been supporting them in relation to another of their adopted children. The adopters were extremely worried that the young person would be abducted. When they talked to the young person, it was obvious that she felt contact with her birth family was out of control. After discussion with the adopters and the young person, it was decided to close down this unregulated contact by changing her phone and closing her Facebook account. A new account was opened after a few months. One of the concerns of the adopters was that, while their daughter's Facebook account was protected and did not reveal personal details, by accessing her friends' accounts personal information could be obtained by implication, i.e. the school she attended.

An adoption social worker

It is possible to prevent your friends' accounts from appearing on your profile - untick the pencil box which appears above your friends' photos on your profile page. This way anyone accessing your profile will not be able to access your friends' accounts as well.

Who are you friends with?

Facebook can suggest possible "friends" to you on the basis of your list of email addresses in another application. So, for instance, if you have ever emailed the foster carer of your adopted child, Facebook might suggest that you make that person a "friend". If you did, and the foster carer had also added a member of the child's birth family as a "friend" (either knowingly or unknowingly), there could be a risk of you being traced through that link.

In some cases, adoptive parents have even received "friends" requests from their child's birth parents, who have managed to trace them on Facebook.

Does your child have a Facebook account? Would she tell you if she did?

If you're not sure, you could try going on Facebook and searching for your child's name. If nothing comes up, she probably doesn't have an account. However, this is not 100 per cent certain. She might have an account that uses a nickname or a shortened version of her name. Or she might even have "blocked" you by name so that you can't see her profile!

- You have to be 13 to have a Facebook account but many younger children set up accounts simply by giving a false date of birth (though if Facebook is notified that this has happened it will close the account in question).

- Setting up an account in a false name and date of birth contravenes Facebook's terms and conditions but is easy to do.

- There have been instances of young people setting up accounts using their birth first name and birth surname and including other details such as their date of birth, to make it easier for any birth relatives to find them. If you find your son or daughter has set up an account like this, it is a sign that they have unanswered questions and are probably searching for their birth family.

Talk about Facebook with your child

- Sit down with your child and talk about her Facebook page and who could view it. Some young people may never have considered changing the default settings or thought about the implications of having their information publicly available.

- Explain to your child (if she doesn't already know) that if her privacy settings are set to "Everyone", then anyone visiting the Facebook site is allowed to view her page.

- If she will let you, sit down together and look at her Facebook profile. Look at it while you are logged in (from your own account) and when you are logged out, to see what is visible in both cases.

- You may be able to see who your child's "friends" are and lots of personal information about her. Some young people include lots of information that could help someone identify them (e.g. date of birth) and locate them (e.g. their school, their town or village).

- Ask your child what she does if someone sends a message asking to become her "friend". Does she accept all requests, even from people she has never heard of? Or does she only accept people she knows and has met in the real world?

- Discuss why some people have to keep their Facebook profile more private than others – e.g. young people who want to apply for a job in a particular profession might not want potential employers to be able to check out their Facebook page and see what they get up to on nights out with their mates. And people who work in, say, the police force or mental health (or schools) might not want to be easily traced on Facebook.

- Explain that, in the same way, someone who has been adopted might not want to be easily traced. Talk about why being adopted means having to do some things differently from your child's friends. Empathise with her about the fact that her life is more complicated.

- Talk to your child about the risk that, without the right privacy settings, she can be contacted out of the blue by a birth relative through Facebook. Ask her how she would feel about this. Perhaps she might want to avoid this because it's not the best way to make this contact?

- If she is receptive, you could suggest other ways she could keep her online identity private (see *Using privacy settings is vital*, p. 45).

- Remind her about what she can do if she wants to know more about her birth relatives or if she wants to make contact (see Chapter 2 of this book). Make sure you show her that you are open to the idea of making contact and that you accept it is something she may want to do.

- The idea of being in control may appeal to her. Explain that having the right privacy settings on Facebook and not accepting random people as "friends" means that she keeps control. It means that she is the one who decides whether and when to have contact. This is better than being taken by surprise when she might not be ready or it is a bad time, e.g. the night before an important exam.

- Talk to your child about the nature of internet communication and how it's easy for people to do or say things on the spur of the moment without thinking, which they might later regret. Remind her how, once you have given someone certain information, you can never get it back.

A word of caution: we never know everything that our children get up to. Remember that, even if your teenager shares their Facebook activity with you and co-operates with all the security measures you suggest, including blocking birth relatives, there's nothing to stop them from setting up a second account which you don't know about. As explained in earlier sections of this book, there is no substitute for being open with your son or daughter and letting them know they can come to you if they have unanswered questions.

> *All I can say is adopters need to be very careful about other people knowing the child's birth family name because even if the family don't do anything, friends at school may do something. We have found other teenagers encouraging him, not really understanding the complexity of it all, and so making him even more vulnerable. I think if some of them had known his birth name they might have done some digging too.*
>
> AN ADOPTIVE PARENT

Getting Facebook to take action

- Facebook is a multinational company based in the United States – where the US Constitution guarantees the right to "free speech".

- Its corporate culture emphasises the value of free speech and freedom from regulation rather than privacy and safeguarding children.

- Facebook is likely to have limited understanding of adoption issues and therefore may not understand or be prepared to respond to adoptive parents' concerns.

- Issues of unregulated contact or birth parents posting inappropriate material do not fit neatly into the usual categories of Facebook "offences", e.g. posting pornographic images or online grooming by paedophiles.

Facebook is resistant to getting involved in any disputes about material which people have posted onto their pages.

Complaining to social networking sites

> *We offer email support for Facebook because it enables us to most effectively and efficiently serve our over 400 million users worldwide. Through emails submitted using the contact forms in our Help Centre, our User Operations team is able to veryify the account owner via his or her*

*email address and use automated methods to prioritise requests, making
sure we're handling the most critical requests first. We also provide report
links throughout the site.*

A SPOKESWOMAN FROM FACEBOOK IN THE UK

Complaining to a social networking site can be a frustrating business. The European
Commission looked at the policy and practice of 25 social networking sites across
Europe that signed up to its Safer Social Networking Principles last year. It found that
just nine out of 22 websites responded to complaints submitted by their users.

Many parents and social work professionals have found it impossible to complain
to Facebook – though there have been some successes. Some families have had
long battles with Facebook – one family ended up writing direct to Facebook's chief
executive in California before they finally achieved the result they wanted. Some
parents suggest writing direct to the head office of the offending site rather than
using their reporting system. Send as much information as you can and be prepared
to persevere. Sometimes children's services have the same difficulty getting social
networking sites to take action.

The Children's Charities Coalition on Internet Safety (CCCIS) has lobbied on this issue. Its
Digital Manifesto refers to concerns about the unresponsiveness of social networking
sites to complaints. One example of this was an adoption case where the birth parent
had posted a request for information about the child's whereabouts. The site where
the request was posted insisted that the adoptive parents had to raise the matter with
them directly, rather than through the adoption agency.

*The site refused to respond to an intercession by the adoption agency
that had placed the child. It should be possible for sites to respond to
reports or requests from trusted third parties, for example, an adoption
agency or a recognised child protection agency acting in good faith,
rather than insisting that the adoptive parents identify themselves. That
could compromise the child's anonymity and, with it, the child's security.
This example reflects poorly on the flexibility, responsiveness or even
understanding of and interest in child protection issues of those running
such sites.*

DIGITAL MANIFESTO, CCCIS

Reporting suspicious behaviour

In April 2010 Facebook agreed to set up new measures to allow users to report
unwanted or suspicious behaviour directly to child protection organisations. Other sites,
such as Bebo and MySpace, include a button which links directly to CCOP (Child Online
Exploitation and Protection Unit). Users can press the button if they feel threatened or

worried by somebody who has made contact. Discussions are continuing and adoptive parents need to keep up with developments so they can give the most up-to-date advice to their children.

Photographs and your family

Uploading photographs and videos to the internet

People can share their photographs and videos with others through websites such as YouTube and Flickr as well as on their Facebook or other social networking profile page and in photo albums on their page. Many mobile phones can now take photographs and videos too. All of this has implications for adoptive families.

Letterbox photographs

In many adoptions, adoptive parents agree to send the birth relatives photographs of their children (usually as part of letterbox contact, with names and addresses withheld). Increasingly, agencies are deciding to stop asking for photographs to be provided by the adoptive parents as part of letterbox contact in every case, because of the number of cases in which birth parents have then posted the photographs on their Facebook pages (see below). There is also the risk that a photograph provided as part of letterbox contact could be a way of tracing a child. However, it is important that these decisions are proportionate to the risk and are based on proper risk assessments.

In most cases, sending photographs does not present a problem and adoptive parents see it as something they want to do for the birth parents.

If your child's birth parents request photographs and you don't want to provide them (or if you want to stop providing them), discuss this with your adoption agency. It is important that everyone involved understands the nature of the request and the decisions taken about it. You might want to write a letter and ask for this to be kept in your child's file.

Misuse of children's photographs

It is an unpleasant and distressing truth that children's photographs, taken by people who love them, can be misused by others. Some adoptive parents are understandably uneasy about the possibility of photographs of their children being used inappropriately.

The NSPCC has issued guidance for people who run sports clubs about the possible misuse of photographs of children. It says that in some cases photographs have been found to be digitally altered and have surfaced in child pornography on the internet. There are also reports that photographs of children are used as "trading cards" by sex offenders in prison. These cases highlight the importance of clear and well-informed risk assessments. Letterbox services may have a policy that they will not pass on children's photographs to known or convicted sex offenders.

Birth relatives and Facebook photos

There have been many cases in which birth relatives have displayed photographs of their children on their Facebook profiles. Sometimes these are photographs taken before the adoption; sometimes they have been supplied as part of letterbox contact.

Not surprisingly, it can be a shock for adoptive parents to find a photo of their child on a birth parent's Facebook page.

- Some feel angry or upset that their child appears on the profile page of the person who neglected or abused him, or simply feel sorry for the birth parent.

- In some cases, a birth parent presents a false picture of a happy family life, perhaps even implying that the children are still with her.

- Adoptive parents may feel it is an invasion of their child's privacy to have his photograph used in this way.

- The child (if he is old enough) could search and come across the photograph of himself, which could be disturbing or upsetting for him.

What can be done?

What can you do if a birth parent is using the internet to post inappropriate messages or displaying a photograph of your child on their Facebook page? There will be many occasions when it simply may not have occurred to the birth relative that there is anything wrong or inappropriate in what they are doing. Many people automatically post any and all of their photographs on their Facebook page for others to see. Sometimes, birth parents may post information or photographs on the internet out of a need to know what has happened to the child or in an attempt to trace or make contact. In a few cases, they may be seeking this contact for dangerous purposes.

The placing adoption agency or adoption support service should be prepared to help you deal with this. For instance, if you have indirect contact with the birth relative who has posted a photograph or message that you feel is inappropriate, you can ask whoever manages the letterbox contact to get in touch with the birth relative and ask them to take down the photograph.

> *I would like to see the social worker in our case send a letter to say that, on checking on Facebook, she noticed the photograph of M and that the birth mother is no longer able to use M's photograph in this way and perhaps even that further comments could result in the local authority asking Facebook to shut down her account.*

AN ADOPTIVE MOTHER

If the photograph is one you have supplied as part of letterbox contact, you can point out that the photograph is yours. In this situation, many birth parents will back down, realising that you could well refuse to provide any more letterbox photographs if they don't agree to remove it. However, some are less co-operative. You may have a battle on your hands, particularly if the photograph is their own.

Can you get Facebook to take action?

What can be done via Facebook if adoptive parents object to birth relatives posting photographs that they have received through letterbox contact?

> *In certain cases, we may remove photos of young children when we receive a report from a parent or legal guardian that the photos are not authorised.*

A SPOKESWOMAN FOR FACEBOOK IN THE UK

If birth parents looking for their children post photos and messages trying to find the child, can Facebook do anything to protect the identity of the child?

> *It's a violation of our policies to post personal information about a private individual in a public space without that person's consent. We remove content that does this when it's reported to us by our users.*

A SPOKESWOMAN FOR FACEBOOK IN THE UK

THE FOLLOWING GENERAL ADVICE ABOUT PHOTOGRAPHS IS GIVEN ON FACEBOOK ITSELF:

What do I do if someone has posted an objectionable photo on Facebook?

You can anonymously report photos that violate our Terms of Use (e.g. pornography or copyrighted images) by clicking on the "Report this photo" link below the picture. Facebook reviews these complaints and takes down photos as necessary.

What can I do if someone has posted a photo of me that I don't like?

Facebook will only remove photos that violate our Terms of Use (e.g. pornography or copyrighted images). However, there are some things you can do if you don't like a photo of you on the site:

1. To remove your name from a particular photo, simply view the photo and click the "Remove Tag" link next to your name. It will no longer be linked to your Profile.

2. Remember that you can only be tagged in photos by your friends. If you are having problems with someone constantly tagging you in embarrassing photos, just remove them as a friend from the Friends page.

3. If you don't want the photo to be shown at all, please talk to the person who posted it. They should be respectful enough to remove unwanted photos. Unfortunately, Facebook cannot make users remove photos that do not violate our Terms of Use.

Photographs: a way of tracing a child?

There is a risk that a child could be traced via a photograph – either a conventional photograph or an online photograph – if you don't take certain precautions.

If you, your friends or anyone else posts a photograph of your child on the internet, it is possible that the photo could be seen by a birth parent or relative who could recognise the child, if they live in the same area. Or someone might search for the child's name on the internet and then find an online photograph of the child which might serve to confirm their identity. The chances of them identifying the child from the photograph are much greater if the child's name appears with it on a social networking website or if they have access to pages where the child is "tagged" in a photograph. Without the right privacy settings in place, someone searching online for the child's name could be led to the photograph and other details that might reveal his location.

Birth parents may not know the child's new surname. However, an unusual or unusually spelt first name could still be enough to lead them to the child through an internet search (particularly if there are other details which could tie in with what they know about you, e.g. your home town). This is why you need to be careful.

Suppose a birth parent has managed to track down your teenage child's profile page on Facebook. If your child has a photograph of themselves and the name of the town where you live on their Facebook profile, this could make it possible for a determined parent to find them. If your child posts the name of their school, or the venue where they are going to meet friends one evening, the birth parent could wait outside and recognise them from the photograph when they come out. Even if they don't give the name of their school, there may be only one or two secondary schools in the town.

Facial recognition technology

The scope for "finding" people electronically is growing all the time: a new Google service called Goggles uses images rather than words to search the web. At the time of writing, it is not yet available to use for faces – but this could only be a matter of time. Google is considering the privacy implications of this. But facial recognition technology is already here, albeit in its early stages. In future, parents will need to be even more careful with photographs of their children.

Taking precautions

Here are some precautions you can take if there is thought to be a risk for your child if he were identified.

- If you decide you want to post photos online – to share with your family or friends – set your privacy settings to the highest possible level so that only people who are classed as your "friends" can see them.

- Think about the possible implications of school photos, websites and other publications like school magazines.

- If there is any likelihood of online links between birth relatives and your own friends and family or your child's friends, make sure no one "tags" any Facebook photos with your child's (or your) name. Some parents ask their friends and family not to post any photos of their child at all.

- If the birth parents have met you and/or your partner, you may prefer not to have any photographs of yourselves online if you feel there is a risk.

- If your child or teenager is posting photographs online, make sure their privacy settings are set so that only their friends can see them. They may want to avoid including any photographs of themselves in front of obvious locations such as in front of their house or street sign or school.

- For a small number of children for whom significant risks have been identified, parents may need to consider refusing permission when schools and other organisations, e.g. sports clubs, ask for signed parental permission before taking and/or publishing photographs of children or filming them.

- Schools should take precautions not to put looked after and adopted children's security at risk – some schools do not allow any photos or filming at school events, except perhaps for allowing parents to take individual photos of their own child after the play.

- If you feel there is a risk, make sure the school and any sporting or other organisations your child belongs to know that you do not want your child's name to appear on their website, e.g. in reports of sports fixtures, etc. Put this in writing and remind them every new school year.

- You may want to make sure your child does not even appear in any class or school photos, if there's a risk the birth parents know your surname and the area you live in and might be searching for the child.

- If you are supplying photographs through letterbox contact, make sure the photographs do not have any identifying information on them, such as the child wearing their school uniform, street names in the background and so on.

- If you are supplying a photograph taken by a photographer or you had your photos printed at a supermarket, make sure there is no identifying information that could be misused (such as your surname or the photographic studio's address) printed on the back of the photograph.

In all cases, a measured response is what is needed.

Worried about providing photos?

Parents who have concerns about supplying letterbox photographs sometimes do the following:

65

- Supply photographs where it is difficult to make out the child's features – for instance, taken at a distance or in fancy dress or with their face partially obscured by a hat or food, for instance.

- Supply photos taken a year or so ago, so that the child is not so easily recognisable.

- Instead of a photo, supply a picture that the child has drawn of themselves, or their handprint or footprint in paint.

- Provide photographs in a format in which they can't easily be posted on the internet, e.g. in a keyring.

- Tell the birth parents you are putting photographs and mementoes of your child for them in a "memory box" and that your child will be able to give this to them himself, when old enough, if he wants to.

- Agree to provide photographs on condition that the birth parent looks at them in the adoption agency's office and does not take them away (but remember it only takes a moment to take out a mobile phone and take a photo of the photograph).

- Some parents who feel they cannot trust people to keep the photographs safe refuse to provide photos under any circumstances.

CASE STUDY

A seven-year-old girl lived with her aunt (the sister of her birth mother) and her birth mother was allowed indirect contact. On one occasion, the girl's mother went round to the aunt's house when the child was not there, to drop off a present. A few days later, the child's photograph appeared on the birth mother's Facebook page. The aunt recognised the photograph as the one that sat on the mantelpiece in her home – the mother had used her mobile phone to take a photograph of it when she was left alone in the living room for a few minutes.

CASE STUDY

Oxfordshire County Council had concerns about letterbox photos in the case of a three-year-old adopted girl. The local authority felt that, if the girl's birth parents had a photograph of her, they might use the internet and social networking sites to try to find her. It argued that allowing the couple to view a photograph, once a year, at the council's offices was enough to meet any obligation it might have under the Human Rights Act.

The birth parents challenged this and at an Oxford County Court hearing in 2009, a judge ordered the girl's adoptive parents to send an annual letterbox photograph of their daughter to her birth parents.

However, in May 2010 the local authority challenged the ruling at London's Civil Appeal Court and won. The Master of the Rolls, Lord Neuberger, said that the adoptive parents' concerns were genuine and that there was no justification for forcing them to do something they conscientiously and reasonably objected to.

The girl's birth parents will be allowed to view a photograph of her, annually, at the council's offices.

Although anxiety about supplying photographs is understandable, it is worth thinking about the wisdom of taking any extreme actions. In all cases, looking at the risks and balancing the advantages with the disadvantages will be a useful strategy to follow. Where possible, it would be helpful to learn to assess the risks so that any actions you take are well informed and not the result of anxiety, panic or fear.

8 Unmediated contact with birth relatives: managing the consequences

Facebook messages are, of course, far from the ideal route for re-opening contact with birth relatives. Electronic communication lacks the nuances and non-verbal signals that help us to "read" a person and their intentions when we are with them face to face. Making contact with unknown birth relatives – parents or siblings – in this way is clearly fraught with difficulties for an adopted child or young person.

- The things they are communicating are sensitive, distressing and raw. "Instant" messaging is the very opposite of what is needed.

- Emails and instant messages can be blunt and nasty, and contain accusations, recriminations, anger, grief, manipulation or shocking news.

- One or both parties may lack emotional intelligence and any awareness of how the communication could affect the other person.

- One or both parties could be seeking to make contact with a view to blaming, exploiting or abusing the other.

- Miscommunication is common – either party could be left feeling angry and hurt at what has been said, whether they have understood it correctly or not.

- One or both parties may lack literacy skills, which means messages are unclear or ambiguous.

- After online communication, they may be left feeling on a high and excited, or distressed or angry, with no means of letting their feelings out safely.

- After sending an email or text message, there can be an agonising wait during which the person is constantly checking for a reply.

- They may never receive a reply or the person may stop replying, and they are left feeling confused, rejected and perhaps distressed or angry.

If the child or young person hasn't told anyone, she is alone and unsupported as she tries to deal with all of this.

> *One father started sending messages to his daughter which started out pleasantly enough but soon turned intense and unpleasant, with comments like: 'If I can't see you, I'm going to kill myself'.*

Understandably, some birth parents have been missing their children and longing for contact for years. Even if they have had letterbox contact, this is vetted and they may not have been able to tell the child everything they wanted to. If they do manage to make direct contact, they may want to form an intense bond very quickly. This could be overpowering for the young person and may make her feel out of her depth.

In some cases, birth parents have behaved in the following damaging ways after making contact:

- bombarding the young person with texts, emails and phone calls;
- passing on the young person's details to other birth family members, which results in her being contacted by several other members of the birth family;
- undermining the adoption by trying to win the young person's affections;
- rewriting history and denying any responsibility for what happened;
- demonising social services for removing the child;
- trying to persuade the young person to meet them;
- venting their own unhappiness, loneliness and difficulties;
- drawing their child into disputes they are having with their partner or other family members;
- drawing their child into their own damaging behaviour, e.g. drug or alcohol misuse.

Some birth parents, whose children were removed because of abuse, still represent a serious threat. Any contact - even email contact - would be extremely dangerous.

There have been instances where the contact between an adopted child and her birth relatives is hostile, or amounts to harassment. Sadly, in some cases the contact can degenerate into abuse and name-calling, sometimes on both sides, with neither party seemingly able to detach themselves from the situation.

Here are some examples from adoption social workers.

CASE STUDY

A 14-year-old boy found his original birth certificate and traced his birth sister on Facebook. She didn't believe him at first. But her mother was there with her and joined in the Facebook conversation. The mother is in denial about the past - she is telling the boy that social services took him from her because she was feeling "a bit low" and that she didn't do anything wrong. He is now very angry and is saying he wants to go and live with his mother.

CASE STUDY

We have a teenage boy who is social networking with his very large group of siblings and other extended family. One of his siblings contacted him on Facebook and told him that he was about to have a new sibling. He was really worried as his birth mother has 14 children, most of them adopted with different families. The last two babies were removed at birth. Enquiries were made with the local authority where her Facebook page said she was living. They were able to reassure us that there was no pregnancy.

Some time later our teenager remained really concerned that his mother may have moved and "slipped through the net" and have a baby that she is not taking care of, as he had now seen pictures of her on Facebook holding a baby alleged to be hers. (However, all my enquiries inform me the child is not hers.) So not only can young people find their family – they can now be taunted via such sites by birth family members.

· ·

Even when the birth parent is not doing any of these things, simply having the birth parent come back into their life can have a destabilising effect on a vulnerable teenager.

Often the initial approach is followed by a "honeymoon period" during which the child or young person believes that finding the birth parent is the answer to all their problems.

CASE STUDY

· ·

I am the adoptive parent of a 17-year-old. We adopted our daughter ten years ago and she had had no contact with her birth father and no one was aware of his name. Four years into placement, the birth mother divulged the man's name, but nothing was known about him. Last March, just prior to her GCSEs, our daughter came into the kitchen rapturously excited because her father ("my Dad") had contacted her on Facebook.

It had taken him 11 minutes, from the outset, to get in touch with her - he had simply entered her two very distinctive first names, which we had not changed in line with current recommendations, identity needs, etc. He could have been anyone, he could have been a convicted paedophile, or, perhaps worse, an unconvicted one!!

Anyway, it turned out he was OK, just inadequate and thoughtless, but his arrival on the scene threw my daughter's life off track, nearly ended my marriage and has caused my son to move out. She stopped doing any school work so got poor grades at GCSE, treated my husband like dirt, and he can't get over it, and idolised this other man and his entire extended family. I took her to meet her birth father and his present girlfriend and their new baby, our daughter's half-brother, and she has spent a couple of weekends with them. Our daughter has got drunk, beaten me up quite badly, damaged our home and – among other things – spat at my husband.

I can accept the turmoil and identity crisis she is undergoing, but my husband and son cannot. The atmosphere between her and my husband (she had always been a daddy's girl) is very cool.

She is beginning to be more realistic about her birth father since the girlfriend has dumped him and doesn't want him round her baby. She has been able to accept that there is going to be another fatherless child due to his feckless behaviour and she has cooled towards him. However, she now spends nearly all her time on Facebook, like the friends who she used to say needed to "get a life".

She has put on weight, having been super-fit, and is drifting. She feels disloyal to her birth mother who has serious mental health issues, and with whom we have had twice-yearly letterbox contact. But she hasn't bothered to write to her, as she doesn't want to tell her about the emergence of her birth father and doesn't know what else to say.

Contact with other birth relatives

In many cases the initial contact comes from an older or younger brother or sister of the adopted child.

> *I have had one case where adopted children have found each other on Facebook. Luckily these young people had good open relationships with their adoptive mothers and so involved them in what they were doing and it has worked out very positively. In another case, a young adult supported by our looked-after system found her adopted siblings on Facebook. Again, it was fortunate that the young people had good supportive open relationships with the carers and adoptive parents.*
>
> A POST-ADOPTION WORKER

CASE STUDY

My adopted daughter has a half-sister (by a different father), who was born soon after her and who was also adopted as a young baby. The half-sister's adoptive family moved right away from the area after the final adoption order. No letterbox contact was set up. They sent a Christmas card (addresses were allowed to be known) but nothing more. The parents were very security-conscious and were not keen on contact of any kind.

Out of the blue, five years ago, the half-sister rang our home and they spoke for the first time...no social services, just that. She was 13 and our daughter was 16. Then of course the girls started to have internet and mobile phone contact.

The two girls have had very different upbringings and it's an uneasy relationship. This half-sister doesn't seem to want to go down the conventional route to find out about her birth family and is trying to get my daughter to cough up all sorts of information. They go on Facebook a lot and she has been badgering my daughter.

I can't really trust what my daughter tells me, but she says she has NOT told this younger, unsupported person about the information she has about their birth mother...But personally, I would expect my daughter to get a lot of kudos and feelings of superiority out of dangling tit-bits in front of her half sister. Their birth story is a horrible one to come to terms with and I am concerned that this girl is not telling her parents about the information and getting the support she will need. I am wondering if I should call up her adoptive mother and tell her.

Maybe this half-sister has traced the birth mother. With Facebook, it's so easy. I am sure as I can be that my own daughter would not contact her birth mother at the moment. She was very angry and disappointed about the things she found out when we went down the conventional route two years ago.

It seems to me that with the internet and social networking, the already complicated adoption journey is tangling beyond ANYONE's control...and the fallout will be horrendous for many people.

....

In some cases, brothers or sisters still live with or are in contact with the birth parents. Contact with a sibling can rapidly lead to contact with a birth parent. Complex situations can arise, involving several families.

CASE STUDY
....

Sixteen-year-old Amy's adoptive placement had broken down when she was 14. She had letterbox contact with some birth relatives, including her brothers, but not with her mother. She started asking for contact with her birth mother when she left her adoptive family. In spite of her history of abuse and neglect, Amy had an idealised view of her mother. But in fact her mother was a drug user who had been living a rough lifestyle. She looked quite alarming – she was gaunt and unkempt, with few teeth.

Letters were exchanged between Amy and her birth mother. The post-adoption team began to assess and prepare both Amy and her birth mother in advance of any face-to-face meeting. But before the preparations were complete, Amy's birth mother sent her a message on Facebook and they began talking to each other.

Amy had moved from one foster placement to another and had ended up in residential care. Soon after the Facebook contact, Amy's birth mother travelled across the country to the residential home. Because she was 16, staff at the unit complied with Amy's wishes and she left and moved into the mother's flat.

Amy and her mother contacted one of Amy's brothers (who had been adopted), again by Facebook and arranged to meet him. The brother met them in secret, without telling his adoptive parents. He was unsettled by the meeting and didn't want any further contact. When his adoptive parents found out, they were upset and are seeking recourse through the law in an attempt to control the situation. Their relationship with their son is strained as they feel they can't trust him. They also feel very upset and intimidated by the possibility of further Facebook contact from Amy, the mother and other siblings. It's not known if he is still in touch with Amy – if so, it is likely to be on Facebook.

Amy left her birth mother's flat after two months. The birth mother feels angry with Amy for not responding with gratitude to her offer of a home. But they have maintained contact. Unfortunately she is supplying drugs to Amy.

Amy's adoptive parents have tried to maintain a link with Amy and be as supportive as they can but understandably they have mixed emotions.

Understanding the pull of the birth family

To fully understand why your child might want to make contact with her birth family, you need to be able to empathise with her. You probably thought quite a lot about your child's grief and loss when she first came to you. You will have been aware of how strange it must have been for her to join a new family. But, for an adopted child or young person, being in a family that is different from their birth family is something that doesn't go away. Throughout their childhood and adolescence they may live with a feeling of "not fitting in".

Nancy Verrier (2010), in *Coming Home to Self*, writes about this.

> *No matter how nurturing, loving or affluent the adoptive parents may be, living with genetic strangers is a very hard life for a child; he has to spend tremendous amounts of energy trying to fit into a family in which he feels alien.*

She discusses adopted children's experience of growing up in a family in which their own genetic traits (facial features, gestures, body language, temperament and so on) are not reflected back to them:

> *Those of us who have not had to experience this deficit have no idea what it is like to exist day after day with no mirroring of our genetic characteristics...It isn't until they experience the ease of being around their birth families that adopted people even begin to understand it themselves. Despite this difficulty, the main issue for adopted children and young people is that of loss, the loss of the birth mother. If adoption is to be helpful to a child who needs parents, the adoptive parents as well*

as the professionals who work with them will have to first acknowledge the existence of the child's loss and the issues which ensue.

Adoptive parents have to help their child work through the resulting pain. And the most important part of this is validating the child's experience.

But sometimes we don't want to hear anything negative. Instead of validating her experience, our first instinct may be to discount what she is saying, concentrate on our own feelings ('But I love you just as much!') or try to offer reassurance. If, instead, you can listen to her and empathise with her about the difficulty of being adopted, then she will feel understood and will be more likely to share her feelings with you. She will express how she feels only if she knows you are ready to hear it and strong enough to take it.

This idea of the importance of genetics may go some way to explaining the pull of the birth family. This may be a reason for the intensity which is often a feature of the early contact between reunited birth family members.

Genetic attraction

People reunited with birth family members often feel extreme emotions – it is natural and common for people to feel thrilled and excited and develop very strong feelings for their new-found relatives.

Genetic similarity is believed to play a part in what is known as "genetic attraction". Sometimes, newly reunited birth relatives feel as though they can't bear to be away from each other. They are strongly attracted to each other and have a desire to become close. Sometimes this desire for intimacy, combined with the attraction that results from the genetic similarity, feels like sexual desire. This is known as "genetic sexual attraction". In some cases, people cross the line and the relationship becomes sexual. Sex is used as a way to become very close, very quickly. Brothers and sisters in normally-functioning families do not usually develop sexual feelings for each other. But in adoption, they are separated at an early age and the normal dynamic between siblings is disrupted.

Contact initiated through social networking is often marked by very intense contact early on, in contrast to the conventional, mediated route to reunion which allows people time to get to know each other over a longer period. Obviously there is a strong taboo against sexual relationships between family members. Contact and reunion are difficult and complex enough for everyone to deal with even without sexual urges becoming part of the equation. The outcome can be disastrous. In such cases it is important for those involved to have counselling from a specialist service with expertise in this sensitive area.

If your child is in contact (or about to be) with birth relatives

Some adoptive parents have been shocked to discover that their son or daughter has been emailing, texting and phoning birth parents or siblings and even meeting up, all in secret. Sometimes, young people claim they searched simply because they were bored and mildly curious. Sometimes their friends urge them to search, or even start searching on their behalf, without realising the implications.

In some cases, things can move very quickly, from emailing and phoning to meeting up. It can spiral out of control, leaving the young person feeling pressurised and scared.

Or the initial elation can be followed by a huge let-down.

> *A boy and girl adopted into the same family were contacted by an older birth brother. Without telling their adoptive parents, they arranged to travel into London to meet their brother. They were very excited. But within half an hour of meeting up, the brother said he had to leave and that he would he back later. He never came back. They were left feeling bitterly disappointed and rejected.*

Sometimes disillusionment sets in fairly soon when the young person gets to know the birth parents better. Birth relatives may lose interest and be unable to sustain the relationship. In some cases, the young person comes to realise that her birth relatives have difficulties of their own that mean they have little to offer her.

In some cases, the messages and phone calls are, or become, unpleasant, damaging or even abusive. Yet there are cases in which a young person in this situation seems to get locked into a negative cycle in which she is unwilling or seemingly unable to break off or block the contact, in spite of being offered advice and support to do this. Some young people may feel that to do this is somehow to "let them win" or is like running away from the problem. They need to be supported through the emotional trauma and be given every encouragement to develop some sense of control over the situation.

Katie, 16, was given up for adoption at the age of six months by her birth parents, who did not wish to keep her. This is what she says.

CASE STUDY

One day, when I was 14, I found my birth certificate. I used the internet to trace my birth grandparents' address. I wrote to them and my birth father rang me a few days later. I was so excited at first. He made himself seem like a lovely father.

At first it was all 'How are you, my darling daughter?' but the next time it would be abuse and foul language. He would phone every night when he was drunk and rant at me. My birth father is not a nice guy. He and one of my birth sisters send abusive messages to me on Facebook. My birth sister used to email me every day, saying I was dirt and I should die. They try to manipulate me by telling me things that aren't true. Once he put my birth mother on the phone but I could tell she was being forced to talk to me. I was desperate for them to like me even when they rejected me and treated me like dirt. My birth parents had told everyone in the family that I was dead.

I didn't tell my mum for about two months. I was stressed out and throwing up all the time. I don't like lying to my mum. But I wouldn't have wanted to approach her [to find out about the birth family] because I wouldn't have wanted to hurt her feelings.

Once my birth father said to me, 'I know everything that's going on in your life. I've got Facebook right here in front of me', and he started reading from my profile and my mum's profile. It's like stalking - he uses other people's accounts to make contact.

When they ring it destroys me a little bit. But they don't do it that often now. If I hadn't contacted them, I would have lived my life wondering - but now I know the brutal reality. It stops me from ever wanting to know them.

Katie's mum adds:

Katie's birth relatives didn't want contact after the adoption. We had told Katie about her history as she was growing up.

When this contact happened, we went through the history again with Katie but at first she didn't want to believe it. She said: 'That can't be right - you've got it wrong.'

At first we were in a state of panic. We didn't know if they'd turn up here or what they might do to us. While all of this was going on, Katie struggled a lot with all aspects of her life. For a long time I didn't know where to turn for help and I felt incredibly frustrated.

It's my view now that they will always be there. They are part of Katie's life and she has to find a way of coping with it as best she can. It's really hard for Katie and for us but that's how it's got to be.

....

Katie has had some life story work and counselling from an adoption support worker from the local authority adoption support service. She has also been advised about stopping this damaging contact and involving the police, but - for the moment at least - she is choosing not to put an end to the contact. And, as her mother points out, she can be very determined.

Some months after Katie first made contact with her extended birth family, Katie's eldest birth sister, who had left home and moved to a refuge at the age of 15 several years ago, also made contact with Katie through Facebook. The following day, Katie got on a train (without telling her parents at first) and went to the town where she lives, to meet her. Something positive has come out of all the stress and anguish. The two sisters have re-connected and forged a firm friendship, and Katie's adoptive parents can see that this is important to both of them.

How will you know?

A young girl was contacted over the internet by someone asking if she was their daughter. Fortunately she told her adoptive parents and we discussed how to prepare her if this should happen again.

AN ADOPTION SOCIAL WORKER

Your child may confide in you, provided you haven't made it a huge issue or told her not to have any contact with birth relatives.

Sometimes young people don't really expect to find anything when they enter a birth relative's name in a search, then are stunned to find the person. Some feel quite scared and tell their parents at that point.

I dread to think what might have happened if she hadn't told us, and had tried to manage meeting up on her own. She has not had to lie and live secrets, which would have been more difficult for her. I did feel invaded, which I wouldn't have, had the approach been conventional, via an intermediary, giving us time to get used to the idea. I know our initial reaction to the news was not as it should have been, had we been consulted and the timing been more appropriate. It was all too much of a shock.

AN ADOPTIVE MOTHER

But adolescents are notoriously uncommunicative. Your child may be afraid you will be annoyed or hurt, stop the contact or ban her from using her mobile phone or the computer.

Often parents don't find out until the child or young person has had quite a lot of contact, by phone and email as well. Sometimes there has been contact with several members of the extended family. It can be difficult for some young people to find the words to tell their parents that they have been talking to their birth parents. They may be reluctant to admit that they are finding it too much to handle. Instead, they come up with their own ways of revealing what's been happening.

- One girl – accidentally or on purpose? – left a notebook with a "do not open – private" warning in a family room. In the book were details of her contacts with her birth family on Facebook.

- Another young person left his laptop open displaying an email he had had from his birth mother.

- Sometimes parents can only tell there is something wrong because of their child's behaviour and signs of stress: she may seem agitated, her sleep and eating patterns may change, she may be isolated and spending unusually long hours online, often late into the night. She may quickly change the screen content when you come into the room.

> *A 15-year-old boy was having unsupervised communication with his older birth brother, without his adoptive parents' knowledge. His behaviour deteriorated and he became angry and began self-harming, refusing to eat and truanting from school. The communication was proving too demanding for him to cope with and was triggering memories and upsetting feelings from his past.*
>
> AN ADOPTION SOCIAL WORKER

Your initial reaction

If your child tells you she has already had contact with a birth relative, you may be utterly shocked – but try, if you can, to respond in a calm, measured way rather than instinctively reacting with panic or outrage. Far easier said than done, of course. But if you are angry, hostile or upset, or if you talk about stopping her, she may simply resort to doing things behind your back. If you can manage it, ask her about it in a way which shows you understand that she wants to know about her birth family and that you are not blaming her for what has happened.

Pain for parents

As an adoptive parent, you have taken on someone else's child – and over the years you may have borne the brunt of the effects of early trauma on her development. And you may have seen only too clearly how her early experiences have affected many aspects of her personality and her relationships. Over the years, you have done your best to help her recover from her early adverse experiences and to achieve some stability. Once her birth family come back into her life, you may feel that all of this is under threat. It can bring back to the surface some issues you thought you had dealt with at the time of the adoption and put behind you.

It is understandable if the thought of your child meeting her birth parents evokes a welter of emotions for you and your partner: anger, fear, pain, sadness and great anxiety about her wellbeing and your own relationship with her. Often adoptive parents in this situation fear that this contact will drive a wedge between them and their child.

Often the child is thrilled at having found her birth parents and completely wrapped up in the "new" relationship. She is constantly on the internet, emailing or instant-messaging her new-found relatives. All she can think about is her birth family. You feel excluded, disregarded and hurt. It is particularly hard if the birth parents are giving the child a distorted portrayal of past events and your child believes their version.

Sometimes young people even start talking about moving in with their birth family, imagining that this will somehow make their lives better.

Being an adoptive parent is unbearably painful sometimes. Sadly, some children do leave home to be with their birth parents, although it often turns out not to be a sustained relationship. Adoptive parents have said that this makes them feel that she was never really "their" child at all. They say they feel as though they were only looking after her until the birth parent came back.

What to do now?

Suppose your child tells you that she has been in contact with a birth brother or sister or parent. Every situation is unique – with a different history and a unique combination of personalities, problems and opportunities. So there is no one right way to deal with this. Somehow the situation has to be managed. What you do will vary according to your child's age, what she wants, the circumstances and motivations of the birth parents, their personalities and so on. Recognise that your own personality and attitudes are also factors in how ready you are likely to be to consider supporting any further contact.

Although contact may not always have been in your child's best interests, it's important to bear in mind that things do change. Perhaps now is the time. If she initiated the contact herself, the message is that she had needs that were not being met.

Deciding the best way to take things forward isn't easy when you are feeling shocked, upset, lied to, angry, betrayed or afraid. So don't make any knee-jerk decisions. Give yourself a chance to absorb what you have found out and when you have got over the initial shock, try to consider the following.

- Did the initial contact come from a birth relative or from your child?
- How much do you know about the birth parents?
- Do you have any idea of the likely motivation for the contact? (see *Birth relatives*, Chapter 3)
- How much information has the young person given them already (e.g. has she told them her mobile phone number and/or address?
- What are the possible risks?
- What are your possible courses of action?
- What is likely to happen with each of these courses of action?

Some birth parents are dangerous and you may feel that you'd go to the ends of the earth rather than have them anywhere near your child. But if the birth parents do not pose a risk, you may decide that, although you'd rather the contact had not been made in this way, if your child feels strongly that she wants to meet them, you'd rather she did it with your knowledge and support rather than in secret.

Not all birth parents represent a threat and contact may well be something you could manage (for your child's sake) if you had to.

AN ADOPTION SOCIAL WORKER

Managing the contact

Your first instinct may be to ban your child or teenager from using the internet. However, bear in mind that this is likely to antagonise her. If she is angry with you, it will make any dialogue with her very difficult. Banning may be a short-term solution to allow a breathing space and time for discussion about what to do next. But it's not sustainable for long – there are, after all, many ways a teenager can access the internet apart from at home. She can use it at school or college, the library, an internet café, a friend's house, via her mobile phone, and so on and so on. And then she will be doing it without your knowledge and trying to manage the situation on her own, without you being able to offer any support or exercise even minimal control.

Every family's circumstances are different, of course, and everyone has to find their own way through. You may decide to accept that it has happened and try to manage it rather than trying to stop her. That way you at least have a chance of steering her towards doing things sensibly, with the right support and safeguards in place.

To many parents, it seems unjust that a birth parent should make contact when they are not supposed to and then for everyone to simply agree that the contact should continue. There are, of course, good reasons why birth parents are supposed to wait until the child is 18 (16 in Scotland) before requesting contact. If everyone just shrugs their shoulders and says: 'Well, the mother has made contact now so I suppose it might as well continue', what message does that send to the birth parent and to the child?

This is all true, of course. And sometimes parents and social workers can manage to gain the birth parent's and young person's agreement to stop the contact at least temporarily, while everyone takes stock and agrees the way forward. But birth parents and young people may not always toe the line, even if they appear to agree to it. If a young person wants to continue the contact and is determined to do so, she will achieve this one way or another. It is better for you to be involved than for it to go on in secret.

SOME SUGGESTIONS

Not all suggestions will be appropriate for your child or your situation, but these are things that other parents and adoption professionals have done or suggested.

- Tell your child that you will help her to contact her birth parents (if it's safe to do so). If it's appropriate, you can arrange to take her to meet them in a safe environment. Or ask the agency to arrange a supervised meeting in a contact centre. It is likely to be too distressing for you, as an adoptive parent, to be the one who liaises with and sets up contact with birth parents.

- Remind her about her birth family history. Tell her as openly and honestly as you can what happened and why she needed to be adopted, even if she has heard this before. (Sometimes writing it down in a letter is more powerful and she may find reading it easier than hearing it.)

- Challenge any misconceptions she may have about the past. Explain that the birth parents may be blocking out the painful memories themselves. It is all too easy for people to rewrite history and portray themselves in a more favourable light.

- Remind her that once she has information out to them (e.g. about where she lives), she can never take it back.

- You may want to contact the adoption agency that arranged the adoption or post-adoption support in your local authority. Ask whether a senior social worker could meet with your child and explain the physical and emotional risks of direct contact and why contact needs to happen in a safe and neutral environment.

- The social worker may be able to tell her about real-life examples of similar situations where direct contact (without an intermediary) has backfired and gone badly wrong.

- If your child has younger brothers and sisters (of the same parent) who have not yet been in contact with the birth parent, explain to her why you do not want her brothers and sisters to be drawn into the situation or to have their right to privacy compromised.

- After discussions with your local adoption support service, they may be able to get adoption support services where the birth parent lives to engage with him or her. (An agency that was not involved in removing the child might have a better chance of forming a positive relationship.)

- Whoever takes on this work needs to give the birth parent a clear message that the contact should not have happened; and that even if they are allowed some contact with an older child, there must be no contact with younger siblings.

- Let your child know that you will always be there for her.

- Some young people are angry or under the influence of the birth parent and refuse to co-operate with any contact set up by the agency. Even if your child refuses, you may want to go ahead and set up a meeting anyway so that you are providing an opportunity for her to do it safely if she wants. That way, she cannot accuse you of keeping her from her birth parents.

Direct unmediated contact with birth parents is difficult for an adopted child to manage (even if she started it). It is a complex situation in which your child is trying to somehow reconcile her own needs and the needs of her birth parents. She may also experience divided loyalties, at least for a while. Recognise that she might not be able to consider your needs at the moment as much as you would wish.

Professor Gillian Schofield's study on contact between long-term fostered children and their birth families makes this observation:

> *Children were left with the task of moving between the two "parents", managing the amount of information they passed about each to the other and somehow almost certainly managing the two sets of parents' anxiety about each other.*

SCHOFIELD, 2009

As we have seen, there may be times when adopted children and young people feel that they don't fully "belong" in their adoptive family. But when they meet and get to know their birth family they may come to feel that, although they share genetic material, they don't really "belong" with them either. In many cases, the young person's upbringing is likely to have led to big differences between her and her birth family – both the birth parents and any siblings who have stayed with them - in terms of values, culture, attitudes, behaviour, education and perhaps socio-economic standing, as well as everyday likes and dislikes. Sooner or later, if an adopted young person has enough contact with her birth relatives, both she and they may well become aware of a gulf between them. The young person may sense that they are thinking 'you wouldn't have turned out like this if you had stayed with us' - an uncomfortable message for her to have to take on board. There may even be outright rejection, from either party, which can be painful and distressing.

More than ever, your adopted child is likely to need your support as she goes through the process of working out that:

> *I am who I have become, not who I was or who I could have been.*

AN ADOPTED PERSON QUOTED IN SELMAN, 2000

Help and support for adoptive families

Adoptive parents have taken on sometimes hurt and disturbed children, often on the assumption that there would be no contact with the child's birth family until he is an adult.

> *We have just discovered that our children's birth mother has made contact on Facebook. Both our children were under 18 at the time, one still is. In looking for help and advice via the original adoption agency, the local authority from where they came and our current local authority – it is clear that they all share these concerns and yet have no formal procedure for dealing with it. The incredible shock and incandescent rage is slowly subsiding as we have to now work out how to deal with it in the best interests of the boys.*
>
> AN ADOPTIVE MOTHER

When young people are at risk and adoptive families are struggling with the complex and challenging situations that arise from unregulated contact, they need and deserve all the help professionals can give. These situations fall within the remit of adoption support services.

ADOPTION SUPPORT SERVICES

The need for adoption support does not end after placement when a child becomes settled with his adoptive family. As we have seen, new challenges can arise at different stages during childhood and the teenage years. The Adoption and Children Act 2002 (England and Wales) and the Adoption and Children (Scotland) Act 2007 recognised that adopted children and their families may need support at any time in the years after the adoption.

Local authorities (Health and Social Care Trusts in Northern Ireland) are responsible for providing a comprehensive adoption support service in their area. Under the Adoption Support Services Regulations 2005 (England and Wales) and the Adoption Support Services and Allowances (Scotland) Regulations 2009, local authorities must provide a range of support services in their area to people affected by adoption.

Support services that might be relevant in situations involving unmediated contact through social networking could include:

- assistance, including mediation services, in relation to contact between the adopted child and others, including birth parents and birth brothers and sisters;

- help for adoptive parents to ensure the adoptive relationship continues, including respite care and training to meet any special needs the child has;

- help where there is the risk of an adoption arrangement disrupting or when it has actually disrupted;

- counselling, advice and information.

Although adopters have the right to request an assessment of their needs for support services, there is no equivalent right to provision of support. The local authority will decide what support, if any, to provide to the individual making an application based on the assessment of need and resources that are available.

WHOSE RESPONSIBILITY IS IT TO PROVIDE SUPPORT?

The first three years:

Assessing and providing support services remains the responsibility of the local authority that placed the child, for the first three years after the adoption order. (This applies outside Northern Ireland.) This includes responsibility for managing and supporting contact arrangements.

After three years:

After three years, the local authority where the family lives takes over responsibility for assessing and providing support services. However, the placing authority remains responsible for supporting any contact arrangements. (If the placing authority has provided financial support during the first three years, it will also continue to be responsible for this.)

Local authorities may also – at their discretion – provide services to people outside their area when they consider it appropriate.

When children are placed with adopters through a voluntary adoption agency (VAA), it is in the area where the VAA operates, so a range of services will be available via the VAA, in addition to those provided by the local authority where they live. The VAA may also help to negotiate with the local authority for other services the adopters need.

Looking at contact

When social workers are planning for a child who is to be placed for adoption, they have to consider certain factors when exploring whether contact would be likely to promote the child's wellbeing. These factors are equally relevant in an assessment when contact has come about through social networking. They need to consider a number of factors, including: the child's wishes and feelings regarding contact; the birth relatives' relationship with the child, and their health and emotional wellbeing and their current functioning; the views of the carers, and so on. They also need to consider what administrative, practical, financial, emotional or other support (including mediation or supervision) may be needed, at least initially, to facilitate any planned contact.

Many parents would like to see local authorities and agencies taking a more proactive role in stepping in when there are problems with birth parents and Facebook.

> *I feel the local authority needs to make some policy decisions on this and perhaps instead of the adoptive parents monitoring and forcing this issue, they should look to be the monitors. Perhaps policy could even somehow make it illegal to make contact beyond the "contact agreement" without the prior written agreement of the adoptive parents? We really are at a loss as to how to handle this ourselves, but we know we cannot be the instigators here – it has to come from an "authoritative" place.*

AN ADOPTIVE MOTHER

It may be possible for social workers to talk to your child about possible risks and to try to reason with the birth parents and gain their agreement to stop the contact or at least put it on a different footing, in which it is out in the open, supported and supervised.

But it's important to be realistic and understand that there are limits to what social workers can do. Some young people are determined to continue the contact by whatever means they can; and some birth parents are not open to reason.

CASE STUDY

Our eldest adopted child is 16 and we found out a few weeks ago that she had made contact with her birth family via Facebook. They replied to her and they exchanged many emails and texts even though they know there should not be contact until she's 18. This is a huge worry for many reasons. Her birth dad is a very violent man, who now has information about us. We also adopted her two younger siblings, so this also puts them in potential danger and would cause huge emotional problems if they find out.

It has caused huge emotional upheaval for our daughter – it was really easy to make contact with them, but because she'd done it in secret, she had no support to deal with the issues it has raised, until we found out. It is very easy for birth families to say nice things and "reinvent" the past via emails and texts, leaving a very confused 16-year-old who blamed us for everything going wrong in her life.

We are lucky that our adoption agency has been a huge help in dealing with the situation. They advised limiting opportunities for "unsafe" contact in the short term by blocking Facebook from our computer and confiscating her phone – we had already done that. A post-adoption support worker visited us and spelt out very clearly but kindly to our daughter why such contact is really unsafe both emotionally and physically for her and the whole family.

After checking with us, he has said that he could arrange for a supervised contact session or to write and find out any information she would like from them – she's thinking about this.

Our agency have contacted the placing agency, who are planning to visit birth mum. We are pushing hard for them to do the same with birth dad – he has moved to a different area, which makes this more difficult.

An adoptive parent

....

However, many adoptive families don't want to get involved with the agency all over again. They prefer to try to deal with it on their own.

Can you hold Facebook to account?

It's also important to be realistic about what you – and your social worker – will be able to achieve through Facebook itself.

If your child is under 13 and has a Facebook account, notify Facebook – it undertakes to delete accounts of children under 13.

Many adoptive parents have found it difficult to get Facebook to act over issues to do with contact when the child is a willing party to it.

We put the following (true) scenario to Facebook:

> *Adoptive parents who contacted Facebook to have their 15-year-old daughter's birth mother's Facebook account closed because of unregulated contact with their daughter have been told that, as it was their daughter who was contacted (rather than themselves), they are not entitled to make a complaint. They are told that such complaints can only be made by the individual who is the recipient of the messages.*

A spokewoman for Facebook in the UK confirmed that this is indeed the case, unless there is police involvement:

> *We provided extensive privacy settings that allow people to...block individuals with whom they wish to have no contact. This prevents those people from accessing their profile or communicating with them through Facebook. Only the account owner can choose the settings that are right for him or her. Facebook does not make these decisions on people's behalf.*

> *If there is any inappropriate content on a page we will respond, whoever the request comes from. If it is a case of contact, we would respond if this is being dealt with by law enforcement agencies. If the police are not involved, then it is very difficult for us to do anything. If a user is not doing anything against our terms and conditions, then there's nothing that Facebook as a company can do about it.*

> A SPOKESWOMAN FOR FACEBOOK IN THE UK

Can anyone stop this unauthorised contact?

> *The idea of controlled contact is ridiculous. Having met my child's birth mother, I can see why the courts recommended no contact apart from letters. It seems to me that courts don't remove children permanently from their families unless they are at risk, so to then suggest contact during the teen years when they are so vulnerable is very dangerous indeed.*

> AN ADOPTIVE PARENT

Some families feel unsupported by their agency if it does not manage to stop the contact. Social workers may try their best but ultimately this is outside their control – most contact agreements are voluntary. They can write a letter to a birth parent to tell them that Facebook contact is unacceptable as it is outside the original contact agreement. They can try to reason with birth parents and children. But ultimately, if people won't co-operate, they cannot force them to behave in a different way.

Local authorities are becoming more aware of the problem but also aware of the fact that they can't do much about it. They haven't got any power.

If you are afraid your child may be abducted

Obviously, you will discuss your fears with adoption support services.

Reunite (www.reunite.org) has produced a Prevention Guide to assist parents in gathering together information relating to their child if they fear they may be abducted, as well as information which may be required in the event of an abduction. It is aimed at parents who fear their partner/ex-partner might attempt to take the child out of the country, but it would be useful for any parent who fears abduction.

The guide suggests you contact your local Child Protection Co-ordinator at your local authority.

It also advises that, where there is a threat of abduction, parents should consider letting the following people know. Most of these people will know about the procedures of local Safeguarding Boards.

If you or your child have one of the following, consider telling them what you fear, why and what you would like them to do if they see or hear anything suspicious:

- *The midwife*

- *The health visitor*

- *The family doctor*

- *The nursery officer or nursery nurse*

- *The headteacher*

- *The social worker*

- *The registered child minder*

- *The cub, scout, brownie or guide leader*

- *The youth club leader*

You may also think of others.

Remember, tell them of your fears, who can have legitimate contact with your child and, more importantly, who should not.

REUNITE CHILD ABDUCTION PREVENTION GUIDE FOR ENGLAND AND WALES

Can the police do anything?

Making contact is not in itself an offence. There may be a role for the police if:

- there was a court order for no contact;
- the child does not want the contact to continue and sees it as harassment;
- the child's birth relative's messages are threatening or intimidating;
- the child's birth relative has been convicted of sexual offences.

Police have a duty to protect under-16s and other people considered to be "at risk", for instance, because they have a learning disability or mental health issues.

What does the law say about children and young people who run away?

The legal framework

- The law does not generally regard young people under the age of 16 as being able to live independently away from home.

- Anyone who has care of a child without parental responsibility may do what *is reasonable* in all the circumstances to safeguard and promote the child's welfare (Children Act 1989 s3 (5) or Children (Scotland) Act 1995 s5 (1) or Article 6 of the Children (Northern Ireland) Order 1995). It is likely to be "reasonable" to inform the police, or children's services departments, and, if appropriate, their parents, of the child/young person's safety and whereabouts.

- Anyone who "takes or detains" a runaway under 16 without lawful authority may be prosecuted under s2 of the Child Abduction Act 1984 or ss83 and 89 of the Children (Scotland) Act 1995 or Article 70 (5 and 6) of the Children (Northern Ireland) Order 1995. Enforcement might be problematic, however, if the young person has chosen to stay with another adult of his or her own free will.

How the police can deal with it

Several police forces across the country are using "harbouring legislation" to tackle incidences where young people run away or go missing and are found with people considered to be inappropriate – for example, because they are much older or they encourage the young person to stay away from their home. It has been particularly useful for young people who are thought to be at risk of sexual exploitation.

Leicestershire Constabulary is one of the police forces successfully using the legislation in this way and, along with the Crown Prosecution Service, have produced a protocol which describes the approach to be used. The aim is to disrupt the relationship in the first instance, thereby reducing the risks that the young person may be exposed to. In the longer term it aims to reduce repeat incidences of children going missing from home and care.

Sixteen- and 17-year-olds can choose to leave home. If an under-18 goes missing from home, the police may actively look for them if they consider the person to be vulnerable. They will carry out a risk assessment and decide what action (if any) to take on the basis of this. It is difficult to force the young person to come home if the police do not consider them to be in danger.

If a younger child leaves home to be with a birth parent, this could be considered abduction and it may be possible to use the law to get them back.

A 16-year-old girl had run away from her adoptive home to live with her birth parents. The adoptive parents called in the police. The police visited the girl at the birth parents' home to assess the situation and do what is known as a "safe and well" check. Because she was over 16, was found to be safe and well, was not being held against her will and didn't want to come home, the police could do nothing more.

SPOKESWOMAN FROM CEOP, CHILD EXPLOITATION AND ONLINE PROTECTION CENTRE

Child Exploitation and Online Protection Centre (CEOP)

CEOP is a Government enforcement agency and has policing powers. It can take action if a case involving the internet meets its threshold of "likelihood of significant harm" – in other words, it doesn't have to wait for evidence that a crime has been committed. When it is suspected that "grooming" (including by a parent who is a sex offender) is taking place online, it can covertly monitor the online communication and trace the perpetrator. It can then pass the details to the local police force, who will be able to arrest him. Based on the level of risk, in certain cases CEOP can apply to Facebook to access someone's personal data.

Children's services and police can refer cases to CEOP. If you have concerns of this kind and do not feel you have been given the right advice by the agency or the police, you can also approach CEOP as an individual.

Can you go to court to stop Facebook and other forms of contact?

In some cases, adoptive parents go to court to try to resolve situations where there is unmediated contact.

- Contact agreements made at the time of an adoption are usually voluntary and not legally binding. If the agreement was voluntary, making contact is not illegal.

- Courts are reluctant to make contact orders at the time of an adoption hearing, as that would limit the adopter's parental responsibility and ability to change the contact arrangements. Adopters need to be able to make decisions about what is in their child's best interests and this can change over time.

- Voluntary contact agreements cannot be enforced by law. This applies whether either (a) the adopters or (b) the birth parents either (a) do something that is not in the agreement or (b) fail to do something that is in the agreement.

CASE STUDY

Recently we had a case where we had applied for Placement Orders to progress adoption plans for two older children in foster care where the foster carer had been approved and matched as adopter. The birth father had been having direct but supervised contact but during this time mobile phone numbers were exchanged. There then followed a deluge of text messaging leading to Facebook and other email communication and very rapidly the plan for adoption became a non-starter for the older boy. One of the difficulties was the use of this communication for all sorts of promises.

At the initial hearing, the High Court judge took the view that 'It's a free world and they can text as much as they like'. In a subsequent hearing with a different judge, we were able to obtain an order under s.34(4) (of the Children Act 1989) which limited text messaging to one hour per day. I know even this sounds a huge amount but believe me, it is nothing compared to what was going on.

Section 34(4) of the Children Act 1989 refers to children in the care of the local authority. It states:

> *On an application made by the authority or the child, the court may make an order authorising the authority to refuse to allow contact between the child and any person who is mentioned in paragraphs (a) to (d) of subsection (1) (which includes parents and guardians) and is named in the order.*

However, this applies only to *looked after children*. There is a similar provision in sections 58(1) and 17(1)c of the Children (Scotland) Act 1995 and Article 53 in the Children (Northern Ireland) Order 1995.

Once children are adopted, any legal action has to be instigated by the adoptive parents. But in most cases, this is not a helpful route to go down.

One possible legal route is a **Section 8 Prohibited Steps Order** under the Children Act 1989. This is a court order which is usually used in disputes between parents – for instance, to say that one parent may not take the child to see a grandfather who is a sex offender, or may not remove the child from the country.

When it is obvious at the time of the adoption that the birth parents are going to try to get in contact with the child, or if there is trouble between the placement and the adoption order going through, a local authority might suggest taking out a Prohibited Steps Order before the adoption is finalised. The local authority might be prepared to fund this, either at the time or later if it proves necessary.

Once the adoption has gone through, the adoptive parents have parental responsibility for the child. So if they want to take legal action against a birth parent who is contacting the child, it must be the adoptive parents – rather than the local authority – who take the matter to court.

However, this does not happen very often. The court will take into account the child's own wishes, so the chances of success largely depend on whether he wants the contact or not. If he does want it, the chances of getting a court order against the birth parent are slim.

Another possibility is a **court injunction** designed to prevent someone from pestering or harassing another person. This is an option if, for example, the child is being repeatedly contacted or followed by a birth parent.

You will need to seek legal advice from a solicitor about the various options available.

In most cases, adoptive parents decide against going down the route of taking their child's birth parents to court because:

- it feels like a heavy-handed approach and ratchets up the emotional tension;
- it brings them into direct conflict with the birth parents, which could be hard for the child to cope with;
- it could involve disclosing the child's name and address.

It also involves significant costs. You could contact the Legal Services Commission in England and Wales, or in Scotland the Scottish Legal Aid Board, which grant legal aid in certain cases, to see if it can help you. Local authorities may be prepared to consider funding it as part of adoption support.

Talking to other adoptive parents

Adoptive parents can be a huge help to each other in many ways – exchanging information and practical suggestions, and offering understanding and moral support. If you haven't already, you can meet other adoptive parents through support groups, in post-adoption training and of course on the internet.

Adoption UK (www.adoptionuk.org.uk) has a messageboard where adoptive parents can post messages, anonymously, to share their experiences with others and ask or offer advice. Search for messages by subject – e.g. Facebook – and you will see just how many other adoptive families are facing Facebook dilemmas and traumas and how they are helping each other.

I have just joined the messageboard on Adoption UK – it makes me realise why the kids use Facebook!

A SPECIAL GUARDIAN

Dealing with a crisis

Even when adopted children and young people do not have attachment problems and have successfully formed attachments to their adoptive families, there is sometimes a period of rebellion and conflict in adolescence. If a young person is having unmediated contact with birth relatives it can compound this, resulting in a family crisis.

CASE STUDY

Our daughter came to us at the age of six after having suffered sexual abuse in her family. We have had a huge amount of trouble with the birth parents contacting her as soon as she turned 16 last year. I still don't know if she found them or if her mother found her. Our daughter told us she was going to stay with friends but she was at her birth mother's house for three nights. The father is a Schedule 1 offender and both parents have personality disorders. The mother abuses drugs and alcohol and has had more children since, and has been allowed to keep them. There seems to be something that pulls her to her mother. Perhaps she is afraid the younger children are not being looked after properly. It has been a living hell for months and has nearly broken down the placement.

We are getting support – a "team around the child" once a month – but all the police and post-adoption service will say is that because she's over 16 there's nothing they can do. But emotionally she is functioning at the level of about 12. I can't understand why they can't protect her. The companies running the social networking sites don't care – I haven't even been able to contact Facebook to get her details taken down.

I know all the research about contact and I know kids need contact, but this woman refuses to come to social services to have contact. Maybe with less complex cases than my daughter's it might be possible to prevent some of this by preparing children for contact and going through everything with them. But my daughter has been so damaged by what happened to her that she was never, ever able to attach to us. I am interested in why the authorities seem powerless to police this area.

An adoptive mother

Sometimes young people talk about going off to live with their birth parents and adoptive parents feel they can't get through to them. There is likely to be a period of intense stress and arguments. Even if a young person leaves home for a short time and then returns – which often happens – it is unlikely to be a happy situation for anyone.

The relationship between the young person and their adoptive parents will have taken a hammering and everyone will be feeling raw. When young people get into a cycle of going to their birth parents and then coming home, adoptive parents sometimes feel the situation is untenable. In some cases, they may be driven to desperation and feel ready to give up on a young person who is repeatedly going missing: 'If he wants to go and live with them so badly, he can go'. But of course if the birth parent represents a risk, this is not an option. In this case, social workers will need to encourage the young person to look for an alternative way to live independently if the adoption has broken down.

Sometimes, adoptive parents try everything in their power, but have to accept that there is nothing more they can do. When an adoption breaks down, the adoptive family are likely to feel bereaved and traumatised. They will need time, help and support to get through this.

However bad things get, there is some hope for a more positive outcome in the longer term.

A study by David Howe (1996) of the University of East Anglia shows that many adoptive parents eventually enjoy a more intense, caring and reciprocal relationship with their adoptive child than they would ever have thought possible during their child's difficult and demanding teenage years.

Researchers asked adopters about their current relationships with their grown-up adopted children and the relationships they had with them during adolescence. The study covered 100 children who were at least 23 years old.

Howe categorised the children into three groups, according to the type of care they had experienced before their placement. He asked parents what their children had been like as teenagers, looking at ten measures of adolescent problem behaviour (self-mutilation, eating disorder, lying, truancy, exclusion from school, running away from home, substance abuse, theft from home, offences outside the home and violence against a family member) between the three groups.

At the time of the study, by which time the children were all young adults, 93 per cent of parents reviewed the adoption positively and said relationships with their child were good.

The biggest improvement was found in the group of children who had had adverse experiences in early life and were adopted relatively late, ie after babyhood. Although some of these children had problem behaviours throughout their childhood, adolescence was a time when their angry and challenging behaviour tried their parents to the limit. In this group, only 38 per cent of parents felt that relationships with their child had been positive in adolescence; but 67 per cent reported their current relationship was positive.

Those who did manage to ride the storm (which could last several years) often found that their very insecure, hostile and angry children slowly began to develop an increased sense of security and self-confidence. They stopped fighting their parents and during their 20s, seemingly for

*the first time, were able to accept their love without feeling confused,
angry and anxious.*

HOWE, 1996

In a few cases, relationships did not recover and parents and children had lost contact or conflict continued (although the longer term outcome could still improve for this group as well – the research only followed them up to a certain point in time).

The long-term outcome can be positive

The two examples below show that, in some cases, if birth relatives are reasonable and the situation is managed well, even contact initiated via Facebook can prove to have some beneficial aspects for the child, once the dust has settled.

CASE STUDY

A 14-year-old girl made Facebook contact with a maternal aunt. Unbeknown to her adoptive parents, the girl went to meet her aunt and cousin. Her aunt "treated" her to a tattoo. Her parents were naturally very distressed about this. I met with them and their daughter and we thought of two ways forward. One was that I would contact and try to meet with the aunt. The other was that I would write a history for the adopted girl who wanted more information about her background than her life story book gave. The aunt agreed to meet me and was contrite. She was keen to have contact and clear that this would be on the adopters' terms. She and her daughter have since met for a meal with the adoptive family and this went well. The adoptive parents feel that their daughter is more settled since then. Coming to discuss her story had filled in some gaps and contact with her aunt is currently proving positive. I was hugely impressed by the maturity and generosity of the adoptive parents who realistically decided that once the contact had been made it could not be unmade, and that it was better for them to become involved and manage it than to alienate the aunt and possibly their own daughter.

CASE STUDY

I was contacted by a couple whose 13-year-old daughter had contacted her birth mother on Facebook without telling them. The birth mother had been 16 when she gave birth and had never told her parents or her siblings of the baby's existence. Fortunately she dealt with the issue very well. She asked the child if her parents knew what she was doing. The child lied and said they did. The birth mother said she was not happy about this way of making contact and would get in touch with social services. The child then told her mum what she had done.

The birth mother met with her local post-adoption worker. She was very distressed that her family might find out about the child. We have now established annual letterbox contact and our adopted girl is very happy with this. We have been clear that this cannot be taken further until she is over 18.

An adoption social worker

Coming out the other side

When things are at their worst, try not to give up hope.

- Try to remind yourself that things do change – young people can come to their senses and see things differently, and even the direst situations can turn around, given time.

- Young people mature and people adjust and come to terms with events.

- If the worst happens and your son or daughter does leave for a while, it is vital to keep the door open to them. Keep the lines of communication open if you can – even if it has to be by texts and phone calls. Make sure they have a mobile phone, and keep the credits topped up for them.

> *Unhappy young people have always run away from home. Children can sometimes drift into the underworld, but there may be something in them that will bring them out. Sometimes they come back in their 20s and acknowledge the value of what adopters gave them in their childhood. Adolescence can be so explosive...but it's not the end.*
>
> AN ADOPTION SOCIAL WORKER

> *Our daughter is returning to her practical self and has a college interview next week, so hopefully a year of chaos and instability is now behind us.*
>
> AN ADOPTIVE MOTHER

> *Things are very good for my daughter...we have put a lot of work into supporting her and trying to draw her back into the family after some nightmare years...so far so good....and we love her to smithereens...that's all we have left after being brought very low over a long period of time... the love.*
>
> AN ADOPTIVE MOTHER

We can't tell, right now, exactly where the revolution in social networking will take us or how adoption practice will change as a result. But one thing is certain – a new reality is emerging, which will affect everyone touched by adoption.

When an adopted person traces a birth parent or other relative, it is impossible to predict where it will lead and what the impact on them will be. It is always emotionally charged, even for adopted adults who are settled in life and have a family of their own.

Poet and novelist Jackie Kay met her Nigerian birth father for the first time, aged 42. She writes:

> *No matter whether the experience is positive or negative – it churns you up. It turns your life upside down. It is something that should not be done lightly.*

'MY OTHER DAD IS AN AFRICAN PRINCE', AN ACCOUNT PUBLISHED IN *THE OBSERVER*, 23 MAY 2010

For young people who are struggling with the turbulent emotions and relationships of adolescence, trying to establish their sense of identity and assert their independence, this is even more true.

And to do it through Facebook – in secret, without the support of the people who love you and who know you best – makes this already complex process more risky and more stressful.

It is a shock for adoptive parents when the truth comes out and they often feel as though their worst nightmare is upon them. But many of those who have been through this experience have found that – although it is unquestionably difficult – in time they do get through it, their worst fears do not come to pass and the bond between them and their child need not be permanently changed or damaged.

And for some adopted young people, finding out about the missing piece of their identity, perhaps meeting and getting to know their birth relatives, can be what they need in order to understand themselves better, accept the past and move on in their lives.

Appendix
Privacy settings on Facebook

To get to this section, click on "Account" in the top right-hand corner of your profile page and select "Privacy settings".

This section controls who can see all the content you post on a day-to-day basis (such as status updates, photos and videos). It also includes some things you share about yourself (birthday and contact information) and content others share about you (comments on your posts and photos and videos you've been tagged in). You can set these with one click, and your settings will apply to all the day-to-day content you post in the future. "Customise settings" displays a full list so you can control the privacy level for each setting.

Facebook makes certain information visible to everyone because it wants other people to be able to find and connect with you on Facebook.
- Name and profile picture are visible to everyone so real-world friends can recognise you. These are also displayed when you write on someone's wall.
- Gender is public.
- Networks are visible to everyone so you can see who else is part of your network (and will have access to your information) if you choose "Friends and Networks" for any of your privacy settings.

Other information in this section, including hometown and interests, is visible by default so others will be able to see it unless you change the settings.

This section controls what information is shared with websites and applications, including search engines (applications and websites you and your friends use already have access to your name, profile picture, gender, networks, friend list, user ID, and any other information you share with everyone). When your friends use certain applications and games, this can make some of your information available to others - if you don't want this to happen, use the settings to change it. If you don't want people to be able to find you by using a search engine outside Facebook (e.g. Google), make sure the box 'Enable public search' is not ticked.

The default privacy settings make quite a lot of your information visible to "everyone". You need to change the settings if you want to make your information more private.

If you are not happy with these default settings, you must change them.

You can get more information about this from *A guide to protecting your privacy on Facebook* on www.bbc.co.uk.

References

Childnet, *Young People and Social Networking Services: A Childnet International Research Report*, available at: www.digizen.org

The Futures Company/YouthNet Survey 2009, available at: www.youthnet.org/mediaandcampaigns/pressreleases/hybrid-lives

Howe D (1996) 'Adopters' relationships with their adopted children from adolescence to early adulthood', *Adoption & Fostering*, 20:5, pp 35–43

Neil E (2002) 'Managing face-to-face contact for young adopted children', in Argent H (ed) *Staying Connected*, London: BAAF

Ofcom Media Literacy Audit (2009) available at: www.ofcom.org.uk/advice/media_literacy/medlitpub/medlitpubrss/uk_childrens_ml

Reunite Child Abduction Prevention Guide for England and Wales, http://www.reunite.org/edit/files/Prevention%20Guide%20E&W.pdf

Selman P (ed) (2000) *Intercountry Adoption: Developments, trends and perspectives*, London: BAAF

Schofield G (2009) 'Parenting while apart: the experiences of birth parents of children in long-term foster care', Full Research Report ESRC End of Award Report, RES-000-22-2606. Swindon: ESRC

UK Council for Child Internet Safety (2009) *Click Clever, Click Safe: The first UK child internet safety strategy*

Verrier N (2010) *Coming Home to Self: Healing the primal wound*, London: BAAF

Williams R (2010) 'You worry about their personal safety', *Society Guardian*, 24 March 2010

'I have never met my birth father but now I am following his every move on Facebook', an account published in *The Guardian*, 30 July 2009

Finding out more

There is a huge amount of information available about the general issue of safety on the internet, so that people have the skills, knowledge and understanding to help children and young people to stay safe online.

Advice/information about safety on the internet

Child Exploitation and Online Protection Centre: www.ceop.gov.uk
CEOP provides an internet safety programme for children and young people, called Thinkuknow: www.thinkuknow.co.uk

Many websites used by children and young people incorporate the CEOP "panic button" which allows them to report unacceptable online behaviour by adults, e.g. online grooming by paedophiles. (At the time of writing, Facebook does not incorporate the CEOP panic button on the site.)

Childnet: www.childnet.com
Childnet has produced the CD-ROM *KnowIT All for Parents* (visit www.childnet-int.org/kia) to help parents make sure their child uses the internet safely. It also produces a leaflet for parents and young people on social networking sites, and has resources in Hindi, Punjabi and Urdu.

MyGuide: www.myguide.gov.uk
This is a Government-run online training resource for adults to learn about the internet.

GetNetWise:www.getnetwise.org
This website has a list of internet safety tools for families, with explanations about what each one can do in terms of monitoring, filtering and blocking. For instance, there are various products which will monitor a child's internet use, either with or without his or her knowledge. The website also provides how-to video tutorials, e.g. on setting privacy settings.

www.sophos.com
This website provides lots of useful information about security on the internet.

Ofcom: www.ofcom.org.uk/advice/guides/media
The Ofcom website provides a guide for parents and carers on how to use parental controls and filters to manage children's access to digital TV and internet content.

Ofcom: www.ofcom.org.uk/files/2009/10/location.pdf
A link to Ofcom's guide for parents on how to keep children safe when using location-based services with mobile phones.

Vodafone: http://parents.vodafone.com/ locationservices
This is a link to Vodafone's parents' guide to location services.

Internet Watch Foundation: www.iwf.org.uk
This website enables internet users to report online child pornography.

Get Safe Online: www.getsafeonline.org
A joint initiative between the Government, law enforcement and the business and public sectors, which provides free, independent, user-friendly advice about using the internet safely.

NSPCC/Sport England: www.nspcc.org.uk/Inform/cpsu/Resources/Briefings/briefings_wda60650.html
Guidance produced jointly by NSPCC and Sport England for sports clubs and sport governing bodies that gives advice on the use of photographs of children and also how to use social networking and other websites safely.

Reunite: www.reunite.org
Reunite produces a guide on what to do if you fear your child is at risk of abduction. The guide mostly concerns international abduction but has useful information for anyone afraid of their child being abducted. The guide can be seen at: www.reunite.org/edit/files/Prevention%20Guide%20E&W.pdf.

Advice/information about adoption, contact and reunion

BAAF
Head Office
Saffron House
6-10 Kirby Street
London
EC1N 8TS
Tel: 020 7421 2600
www.baaf.org.uk

BAAF Cymru: Tel 029 2076 1155
BAAF Northern Ireland: Tel 028 9031 5494
BAAF Scotland: Tel 0131 226 9270

Adoption UK
Linden House
55 The Green
South Bar Street
Banbury OX16 9AB
Tel: 01295 752240
www.adoptionuk.org
Adoption UK has a number of regional offices throughout the UK.

Supporting adults affected by adoption – NORCAP
112 Church Road
Wheatley

Oxfordshire OX33 1LU
Tel: 01865 875000
www.norcap.org.uk

Adoption contact registers

The Adoption Contact Register
Room C202, General Register Office
Trafalgar Road
Southport PR8 2HH
Tel: 0151 471 4252
www.gro.gov.uk
For adoptions that took place in England and Wales

Birthlink
21 Castle Street
Edinburgh EH2 3DN
Tel: 0131 225 6441
www.birthlink.org.uk
For adoptions that took place in Scotland

General Register Office
Oxford House, 49–55 Chichester Street
Belfast BT1 4HL
Tel: 028 9151 3101
www.groni.gov.uk
For adoptions that took place in Northern Ireland

Post-adoption centres

England and Wales

All local authorities in England and Wales have an Adoption Support Adviser, who can give advice to people affected by adoption, and direct you to post-adoption centres.

Scotland and Northern Ireland

Birthlink
21 Castle Street
Edinburgh EH2 3DN
Tel: 0131 225 6441
www.birthlink.org.uk

Barnardo's Scottish Adoption Advice Services
Suite 5/3, Skypark SP5
45 Finnieston Street
Glasgow G3 8JU
Tel: 0141 248 7530
www.barnardos.org.uk/saas.htm

Adoption Routes
Ground Floor
Unit 2, 18 Heron Road
Belfast BT3 9LE
Tel: 028 90736080
www.adoptionroutes.co.uk

Family Care Society
511 Ormeau Road
Belfast BT7 3GS
Tel: 028 90691133
www.familycaresociety.net/

Useful books

All the books listed below are available from BAAF – visit www.baaf.org.uk or call 020 7421 2604 to order.

Marjorie Morrison (2007) *Talking about Adoption to your Adopted Child: A guide for adoptive parents*, London: BAAF
This popular guide outlines the whys, wheres and hows of telling the truth about an adopted child's origins. The multitude of practical ideas for talking to children of all ages are based on the experience of many people who have been adopted, and adoptive parents.

Renée Wolfs (2008) *Adoption Conversations: What, when and how to tell*, London: BAAF
This in-depth practical guide explores the questions adopted children are likely to ask at different ages, with suggestions for helpful explanations set out in possible dialogues. Although the guide focuses primarily on children adopted from abroad, the practical advice given is applicable to any adopted child.

Renée Wolfs (2010) *More Adoption Conversations: What, when and how to tell*, London: BAAF
A sequel to *Adoption Conversations*, this in-depth practical guide explores the problems that adopted teenagers are likely to confront, with suggestions for helpful solutions and communication methods. Although the guide focuses primarily on children adopted from abroad, the practical advice given is applicable to any adopted young person.

Liz Trinder, Julia Feast and David Howe (2004) *The Adoption Reunion Handbook*, London: John Wiley & Sons
This handbook draws on the real-life experiences of adopted people who have searched for, and been reunited with, birth relatives. Comprehensive advice is offered on how to begin searching, what to expect emotionally, the legal framework, and other issues.